Dragoon helmet plate of 1800. This is the first known distinctive branch insignia authorized for the Army. It shows a mounted dragoon in the act of charging. THE SMITHSONIAN INSTITUTION

A symbolic portrayal of the U.S. Army's long and distinguished history

UNIFORMS *of the* ARMY

Here is the fascinating story of what American soldiers have worn from the Revolution to the present day. It describes not only the "how" of Army dress, but also the "why," offering vivid insights into military life through the ages. Author Robert H. Rankin, a Colonel in the U. S. Marine Corps, shows that fighting men seldom have actually dressed the way they appear on recruitment posters. The Indian fighters of the western plains, for example, cut very different figures from those portrayed on the television screen. They may have been the most uncomfortably dressed fighters in American history.

UNIFORMS
of the
ARMY

by Colonel Robert H. Rankin

G. P. Putnam's Sons   New York

For Patti and Robin

PUBLISHED SIMULTANEOUSLY IN THE DOMINION OF
CANADA BY LONGMANS CANADA LIMITED, TORONTO
LIBRARY OF CONGRESS CATALOG CARD NUMBER: 67-24165
PRINTED IN THE UNITED STATES OF AMERICA
Book design by Diana Klemin

ACKNOWLEDGMENTS

As is the case in the writing of most nonfiction, and most certainly as is the case in the writing of history, this book is the result of cooperation extended by many people and organizations. Among those were:

Colonel Grover Heiman, USAF, Chief, Magazine and Books Division; Lieutenant Colonel Charles W. Burtyk, Jr., USA, Chief, Magazine Branch, and Lieutenant Colonel Robert A. Webb, USAF, Chief, Book Branch, all of the Directorate for Public Information Department, Department of Defense.

Gerald C. Stowe, Curator, West Point Museum; Edgar M. Howell, Curator, Division of Military History, The Smithsonian Institution; Lieutenant Colonel Marion Kennedy, ANC, Procurement Division, Director of Manpower, Office of the Deputy Chief of Staff, Department of the Army; Major Doris H. Ledbetter, ANC, Officer Procurement Branch, Personnel and Training Directorate, Office of the Surgeon General, Department of the Army; Miss Florence Oblensky, Assistant Chief for Press, Technical Liaison Division, Administrative and Support Services, Office of the Surgeon General, Department of the Army.

Lieutenant Colonel Donald A. Synnott, Executive Officer, Office of the Provost Marshal General; Major John T. Alexander, Assistant Executive Officer, Office of the Provost Marshal General; Lieutenant Colonel Samuel R. Loboda, Leader, The United States Army Band; Captain Gilbert Mitchell, Jr., Assistant Leader, The United States Army Band; Chief Warrant Officer Chester H. Heinzel, Adjutant, The United States Army Band; Specialist 7 Eugene L. Drifmeyer, The United States Army Band; Specialist 6 Stanley Kline, The United States Army Band; Lieutenant Colonel Mary E. Kelly, WAC, Assistant Director, the Women's Army Corps; Lieutenant Colonel Carol H. Williams, WAC, Executive Director, Office of the Director of the Women's Army Corps.

Lieutenant Colonel Merle C. Lewey, Acting Chief, Audio-Visual Branch, Office of the Chief of Information, Department of the Army; Mrs. Edna Curcio, Photo Researcher, Office of the Chief of Information, Department of the Army; Mrs. Donna H. Traxler, Reference Service Branch, Photographic Records Division, United States Army Photographic Agency; First Lieutenant Joseph P. McLaughlin, Jr., Public Information Officer, Headquarters, 1st Battalion (Reinforced), 3rd Infantry Regiment (The Old Guard); Lieutenant Colonel David L. Daub, Enlisted Branch, Procurement Division, Director of Manpower, Office of the Deputy Chief of Staff, Department of the Army; Major F. R. Marshall, Uniforms and Heraldrics, Personnel Service Division, Director Military Personnel, Deputy Chief of Staff, Department of the Army; Chaplain (Lieutenant Colonel) Clayton E. Day, Office of the Chief of Chaplains, Department of the Army.

W. B. Greenwood and Fred Meigs of the Navy Library, Washington, D. C., and Norm Flayderman, New Milford, Connecticut, were especially helpful at all times.

Considerable assistance was also extended by Cora Ford, Mary Snyder, Lieutenant Colonel Isaac P. Cocke, Major William H. Lenny, Albert Loeffler and Bartlett Hawkins, all of National Headquarters, Selective Service System.

Roger C. Taylor, Editorial Director, and Joyce Atwood, Assistant Editor, United States Naval Institute, Annapolis, Maryland, are due special thanks for their thoughtful cooperation.

Colonel Allan G. Crist, Editor of the *National Guardsman,* and the National Guard Association of the United States very kindly gave permission for the use of certain materials used in my articles on Army uniforms which appeared in the *National Guardsman.*

Finally, John Richards, President of Potomac Arms Corporation, Alexandria, Virginia, very generously cooperated in the project by making many research materials available.

Contents

INTRODUCTION

The subject of military history has become increasingly popular during recent years. Before World War II only a few specialists worked in the field. Since then, however, vast numbers of people have become interested in the subject. Intensive research has uncovered a wealth of material, with the result that numerous ideas once known as fact now have been discounted or modified greatly.

The military uniform is of particular interest to many. Specialized writings have appeared in this field, ranging from detailed discussions of differences in buttons to learned papers on the development of military headdress. This book attempts to break away from a highly specialized treatment of uniforms which would be of interest solely to scholars. It is intended primarily for the general reader.

All illustrations used are *Official U. S. Army*, except where noted otherwise. In this connection, attention is invited to the use of color plates by H. Charles McBarron from the series published by the U. S. Government Printing Office for the U. S. Army.

Since Army regulations are constantly subject to change, it is entirely possible that some modifications may occur in uniforms between the time the manuscript is written and the date of publication.

A note as to sources appears at the end of the book.

Robert H. Rankin
Colonel, U.S. Marine Corps
Washington, D.C.

UNIFORMS *of the* ARMY

I

In the Beginning

Although warfare is one of mankind's oldest activities, men have worn military uniforms only for a few hundred years.

In earlier times there were occasional attempts to put the fighting man in some kind of uniform. We know, for example, that Roman legionnaires were dressed alike in helmet and breastplate. Generally, however, until comparatively recent times men went to war in whatever clothing they happened to have.

A chief reason for the development of the uniform was to enable a soldier to identify, quickly and easily, friend from foe in the heat of battle. For this purpose in the age of knightly combat, English knights wore the red cross of St. George on a white surcoat covering their armor, while their Scot foes wore a white St. Andrew's cross on a blue surcoat.

As far as is known, the first military unit to be *completely* uniformed was the Yeomen of the Guard of England's Henry VII, late in the fifteenth century. Not long afterward that versatile genius Michelangelo designed a complete uniform for the Papal Guard. Interestingly, these two units today wear almost the same uniform that they did then.

The first uniform regulation of record was issued in the sixteenth century by Henry VIII of England, who ordered the Earl of

Members of the Yeoman of the Guard, a unit organized by England's Henry VII in 1485, today wear a uniform little changed from that of Henry's reign. COURTESY OF THE NATIONAL GUARDSMAN

Shrewsbury to raise an army and clothe its soldiers in blue breeches and a blue coat trimmed with red. He directed that the soldiers wear a blue stocking on the left leg and a red stocking on the right.

Before the seventeenth century, armed forces usually were maintained only in times of emergency. During the latter half of that century the development of commerce and industry led to the establishment of strong central governments. This in turn resulted in the formation of standing armies kept under arms and ready to serve the state at any time. Meanwhile, the development of large-scale cloth manufacturing and improved financial conditions of governments permitted the purchase of uniform clothing in large quantities. Thus uniforms, much as we know them today, came into being.

Nations began adopting colors for their uniforms which would be associated with them for many years to come. The French and Austrians chose white. The British adopted red or scarlet. The Germans wore blue; the Russians green. Individual regiments were identified by the color of the trim, of the cuffs, and the color and spacing of buttons.

Some of the early uniforms were fantastic in design. Soldiers were dressed like toys and drilled like puppets. Frederick the Great of Prussia began this folly, and George II of England furthered it. When King George came to the throne from the Duchy of Hanover, a province of Germany, the British soldier's uniform was fairly sensible. Basically it consisted of a long red coat, buttoned back from the front for ease in marching, knee breeches that fastened below the knee, long, heavy wool stockings, and heavy shoes. The hat was a black affair turned up on three sides in the tricornered style so often associated with the early American Army. Various colored trim was used to identify the different units.

But King George ordered impractical changes. The comfortable stockings were discarded in favor of extremely uncomfortable and impractical leather spatterdashes—long, tight leggings, buttoning up the side, which extended to mid-thigh. The coats were now buttoned tightly about the throat, enclosing a stout leather collar designed to make the soldier face to the front and to prevent him from lowering his chin at any time.

Brightly colored uniforms eventually were abandoned because they made good targets for enemy sharpshooters. A striking example was the disastrous defeat of British General Braddock's troops in their expedition through the American wilderness against Fort Duquesne in 1755. The British regulars in their bright red coats were easy targets for the French and Indian marksmen hidden in trees and underbrush. Colonial troops accompanying the British were clad in dark hunting dress which blended with the forest background and, as a result, suffered fewer casualties.

Several considerations must go into the design of a uniform. The dress uniform should possess style, dignity, and reflect the tradition of the service. It should readily set the soldier apart from the civilian. The combat uniform should be comfortable, durable, and blend with the background against which it is worn. It is of prime importance that the uniform create

The Papal Guard, first raised in the sixteenth century, wears today essentially the same uniform first designed for it by that versatile genius Michelangelo. COURTESY OF THE NATIONAL GUARDSMAN

15

a sense of manliness and morale. No matter how efficient the fighting man, he is a human being and entitled to be treated as such. A smart-looking uniform helps him retain his self-respect.

In times past the soldier often was considered an automaton. He was provided with but *one* uniform for both dress and combat. Comfort and utility often were sacrificed for parade-ground smartness, thus for decades British soldiers wore tight-fitting red woolen coats while fighting in the stifling heat of Africa and India. Today the soldier is provided with smart uniforms for dress and general duty, as well as a practical and comfortable combat uniform.

The development of titles of rank accompanied the development of the uniforms. Many of the titles are of Latin origin. General is from *generalis,* which refers to one who is in charge of many. In the very early days of organized armies when a king did not choose to lead his troops personally, he appointed a captain general to act for him. Captain is from the Latin *caput,* meaning one with authority. This officer in turn was assisted by a lieutenant general, an officer who took over the command when his senior was not present. Lieutenant, the first part of this title, derives from *locus* (place) and *tenens* (holding), one who holds the place of his senior.

Next in command was the sergeant major general. Sergeant derives from the French *sergent* and the Latin *serviens,* denoting one who serves. Major originated in the Latin *magnus,* meaning an individual who takes charge. These titles were modified over the years and the words "captain" and "sergeant" were dropped, leaving in

order of descending rank: general, lieutenant general, and major general. As a need for more ranks developed it was decided to assign the title of "major" to the officer acting as the executive officer of a regiment, and the title of "sergeant major" to the senior noncommissioned officer of the outfit. Thus, although a lieutenant general outranks a major general, a major outranks a lieutenant.

Brigadier is from the Italian *bigare,* which means to fight. Consequently a brigadier general is one who commands a fighting unit. A colonel, in modern armies usually the actual commanding officer of a regiment and immediately junior to a brigadier general, receives his title from *colonello,* an Italian word denoting the leader of a column.

The title of corporal originated in the French word *caporal* (from the Latin *capodi*), denoting the leader of a small group. In modern times a corporal is a noncommissioned officer in charge of a squad. The title of lance corporal comes from medieval days when the word *lance,* in addition to meaning a weapon, also meant a small fighting unit. The senior soldier in such a unit was known as a lance corporal. Today this is the noncommissioned rank between corporal and private first class.

The word private derives from *privo,* a Latin word meaning an individual, while soldier stems from *solidus,* Latin for a man of skill in the profession of arms. Soldier may also be traced to the Latin *solidarie,* an individual hired to fight for money (*soldi*).

The uniforms of militarily successful nations often are copied by others. After the

16

success of the French Army in the Italian War of 1859–1861, many nations — including the United States — adopted a French-style uniform complete with *kepi* (a cap with a round flat top sloping toward the front). Following the Franco-Prussian War of 1870, when the Prussians soundly trounced the French, the United States and other nations hastened to copy the uniform of the victorious Prussians, even adopting the *pickelhaube,* or spiked helmet. After World War I, British Army styles, including the roll-collar coat, shirt and tie, Sam Browne belt, and smartly tailored breeches with boots and spurs, were adopted by many countries.

For several reasons, one cannot be positive about the *exact* appearance of many early uniforms: the older uniform regulations are vague as to details. Word meanings have changed over the years. Uniforms often were made locally by tailors who were less than masters of their trade. Cloth of exactly the prescribed shade and texture was not always available. Ideas as to style and fashion vary greatly. Design which is considered fashionable today would have seemed impossible years ago.

Contemporary drawings and paintings often are of doubtful assistance, for the artist frequently took considerable license, adding or changing details to suit his fancy. Each year finds historians possessing more details, but the story of uniforms is still incomplete.

Even today, the military artist sometimes is inclined to portray the fighting men of bygone eras as too immaculately groomed and uniformed. Today, also, most of our fighting men don't measure up to the im-maculate standards depicted on recruiting posters. In the following pages, whenever possible, the idealized artists' pictures of uniforms are accompanied by photographs to show how the soldier usually looked.

Various kinds of uniforms worn by independent organizations, 1774-1775. U. S. ARMY PHOTOGRAPH

2

From the Revolution to the Civil War

The first uniforms in this country consisted of the leather coat, steel cuirass, breeches, long wool stockings, heavy shoes, and pot helmet of the early explorers and colonists. Then followed the French in their white and blue uniforms, and the redcoated British regulars sent to America to fight the Indians and eventually the colonists.

But what of the American Army? Many people think that American troops during the Revolutionary War were uniformed in smartly tailored buff and blue. Although General George Washington and his staff wore uniforms approximating this idea, the typical soldier of the age rarely was so well dressed.

On July 3, 1775, Washington took command of the Continental Army. It would not become the United States Army until a year and a day later on July 4, 1776. Probably no general ever commanded more motley-looking troops. There were almost as many different uniforms as units. The colonies, soon to become states, sent their militia contingents, which were variously uniformed. In addition to the militia were the independent companies, whose members bought their own uniforms — all sorts of fancy, colorful dress.

The majority of the Massachusetts and Connecticut militia wore scarlet coats. Colonel Shee's 3rd Battalion, Associators of Philadelphia, wore brown coats with white facings, pewter buttons bearing "No 3," buckskin breeches, and a tricorne hat trimmed with white tape. The 13th Pennsylvania Regiment wore a brown coat faced with buff, light-colored breeches, white wool stockings, and a wool hat. The 4th Regiment of Light Dragoons of New Jersey were very colorful, wearing a green cloak with red collar, green coat with red facings, buckskin breeches and a bearskin-trimmed cap.

The prevailing militia uniforms appear to have been blue coats faced with red and buckskin breeches. A facing on a military coat is a lining worn at the edge of the front, at the collar, and at the cuffs. The idea grew out of the old custom of pinning back the long coattails and rolling back the coat sleeves to allow greater freedom of action, thus displaying the lining, which usually was a different color than the coat itself. Long wool hose or buttoned gaiters reaching up to the calf of the leg and sturdy shoes were worn by dismounted troops. Mounted troops wore boots of various styles. Ammunition boxes, bayonets in scabbards, and canteens were suspended from white crossed shoulder belts. Officers wore a sword suspended from a single belt passing over the right shoulder and a waist belt.

A cloth sash was worn under the shoulder belt or under the waist belt, sometimes under both, by officers. The custom of wearing a sash would continue in the American service for many years. Now, however, the sash is worn only by cadet officers at the United States Military Academy at West Point and at lesser military schools.

The use of the sash originated in European armies, probably early in the sixteenth century. At first it was useful as well as decorative. Unfolded, it could be transformed into a serviceable stretcher by inserting a pikestaff through a hem on each side. Thus the wearer could be carried off the field of battle if killed or wounded.

Early American headgear usually was a low crown hat with medium-width brim turned up on three sides. Mounted troops wore a stiff leather cap, much like an oversized jockey or baseball cap, decorated with a horsehair or bearskin crest. Fifers and drummers wore a less elaborate cap.

The inability of the struggling new Government of the United States to supply its Army resulted in soldiers wearing whatever came to hand. Even units originally well uniformed found it almost impossible to replace clothing worn out in active field service. Consequently a great variety of clothing came to be worn, little of which was uniform, including homespun hunting garb and even elegant town clothes. The young Marquis de Lafayette, who came from France to help the infant republic, noted that he even saw officers wearing clothing made from blankets. Frequently the troops were shoeless and almost naked.

The fringed hunting costume was worn by many units from the back country. The frock, sometimes called a rifle shirt, was loose, reaching to the thighs, and ornamented with long fringes. The trousers also were loose-fitting and trimmed with fringe. For summer the costume was made of coarse linen; for winter it was of buckskin. The hat usually was broad brimmed, sometimes turned up on one side or the other, and decorated with a cockade. At times a coonskin cap was worn. This clothing was practical and durable. Furthermore, it was inexpensive and easily procured. At one time General Washington, despairing of doing anything better, recommended that the hunting garb be adopted as the uniform for the Army. Washington noted that the garb also would have psychological value, since it originally was worn only by sharpshooting frontiersmen, and the enemy might suppose that he faced entire companies of sharpshooters. Washington's plan never was carried out, however.

During the dark and trying days of the Revolutionary War many soldiers died from exposure. Poor roads, inexperienced or incompetent officers, and lack of transportation, added to problems of meager supplies. It is a tribute to the fortitude, patriotism, and courage of the early American soldier that he continued to fight on for independence despite a lack of food and clothing.

Washington sensed the need for securing self-respect and respect for authority in his ragged troops. In this spirit he ordered that designation of rank be worn by all entitled to it. He prefaced his order by stating that ". . . as the Continental Army has unfortunately no uniforms and consequently many inconveniences must arise from not

Dragoon helmet plate of 1800. This is the first known distinctive branch insignia authorized for the Army. It shows a mounted dragoon in the act of charging. THE SMITHSONIAN INSTITUTION

Commander in Chief and staff officers, 1799-1802. U. S. ARMY PHOTOGRAPH

being able to distinguish officers from privates, it is desired that some badges of distinction may be provided. . . ."

As commander in chief, Washington wore a light blue ribbon diagonally across his breast and under his coat as his "badge." Major generals and brigadier generals wore a pink ribbon in the same manner, while aides-de-camp wore a green ribbon. Field grade officers — colonels, lieutenant colonels and majors — wore a red or pink cockade on the hat. Captains wore a yellow or buff cockade, lieutenants a green cockade. Sergeants had a red cloth stripe or a red cloth epaulet on the right shoulder. Corporals had the same in green.

An epaulet is a strap extending from the collar to the shoulder seam of the coat, with an oval pad at the outer end. The edges of the pad are decorated with hanging fringe. Epaulets originated as broad metal shoulder defenses worn as a part of armor. With the introduction of firearms and the decline of armor as a defense, epaulets were greatly reduced in size and were made of cloth, serving merely as decorative devices for military uniforms.

In 1779, General Washington hopefully prescribed a uniform consisting basically of a dark blue coat, white waistcoat, and white breeches. All infantry coats were to be lined with white. The infantry of New Hampshire, Massachusetts, Rhode Island, and Connecticut were to have white facings. The coats of the drummers and fifers of these states were to be white faced with blue. New York and New Jersey infantry would have blue coats with buff facings. Drummers and fifers of these two states were to wear buff coats with blue facings.

Pennsylvania, Delaware, Maryland, and Virginia infantry regiments were to wear blue coats with scarlet facings. Drummers and fifers had scarlet coats faced with blue. Finally, the infantry regiments of North Carolina, South Carolina, and Georgia were to have blue coats with blue facings. Drummers and fifers were to have blue coats faced with white.

So difficult were the times, however, that few soldiers ever wore the prescribed uniforms.

The practice of drummers and fifers wearing "reversed" colors — a combination of colors reversed from those worn by the rest of the troops — originated as a convenient means of enabling a commanding officer to spot quickly his musicians, who used their instruments to sound calls of command.

Fifers and drummers composed the entire musical organization of the early American Army. Their purpose, besides playing the various command calls, was to provide music for marching. Usually they were young boys ranging from nine to fourteen years of age who volunteered for this special duty. Although they were not supposed to bear arms, they often displayed courage and daring.

In 1780 General Washington ordered a more positive method of designating rank. Major generals were to wear a gold epaulet on each shoulder, with two gold stars on each. This marks the first appearance of stars to identify general officers, a custom which has been followed ever since. Brigadier generals wore two gold epaulets with one gold star on each. Colonels, lieutenant colonels, and majors wore a gold epaulet on each shoulder without rank device of any kind. Captains wore one gold epaulet without star on the right shoulder. Lieutenants had the same on the left shoulder. Sergeants bore a worsted epaulet on each shoulder; corporals a worsted epaulet on the right shoulder only.

In 1782, regulations provided further that a soldier who had served for three years with bravery, fidelity and good conduct could wear a stripe of "angular form" on the left coat sleeve three inches below the shoulder. For six years of service he could wear two such stripes. These stripes were to be of the same color as the facings of the uniform. It marked the advent of the "service stripes" which still are worn today.

Care of the hair was always a problem in the early Army, since it was both the civil and military custom of the age to wear either a wig or long hair. When wigs were worn it was impossible to have them all the same color in one unit. In order to present a uniform appearance, long hair was powdered and tied at the back of the neck. Each soldier was regularly issued two pounds of flour and a half pound of tallow for the care of his hair. By today's standards, the result was decidedly unpleasant.

A few women served in the American Army during the Revolution, though they were not officially recognized. "Sergeant" Molly Pitcher fought beside her husband during the Battle of Monmouth. When he fell, she stepped into his place to keep his cannon firing. Another woman soldier was Deborah Sampson who, disguised as a man, served in the Continental Army for seven years. She was honorably discharged after being wounded at Tarrytown.

During the Revolutionary War women sometimes were hired in a *civilian* capacity as nurses. In fact, Washington asked Congress for the services of a matron to "supervise the nurses, bedding, etc." and for "nurses to attend the sick and obey the matron's orders." Unhappily, only a few nurses ever were employed. For the most part the sick and the wounded were left to the clumsy mercy of their companions.

Following the Revolutionary War the United States Army almost disappeared. Congress passed a resolution calling for the discharge of all soldiers except 25 privates to guard government property at Fort Pitt (now Pittsburg) and 55 privates to guard military stores at West Point and other military installations. This "army" of 80 men had a captain as its senior officer. In passing the legislation setting up this "force," Congress pointed out that ". . . standing armies in time of peace are inconsistent with the principles of republican government, dangerous to liberties of a free people, and generally converted into destructive engines for establishing despotism. . . ."

But in order to man the frontier forts evacuated by the British, a larger force was needed. Therefore, legislation soon was enacted to call up 700 men for service for one year, together with a proportionate number of officers. This half-hearted measure proved inadequate, and before long it became necessary to increase the size of the Army greatly.

The "new" Army was organized as a *legion,* a type of military organization which was popular during the eighteenth century. The legion was made up of a composite of all combat arms — infantry, artillery and cavalry — under a single command. This made for a highly flexible and mobile outfit, since it was entirely self-contained. Instead of regiments the legion was divided into *sub-legions.* Each of these smaller units was commanded by a brigadier. It consisted of two infantry battalions, one rifle battalion, one troop of dragoons, and one company of artillery. Each sub-legion was identified by distinctive insignia. During this particular period red facings were introduced for infantry and yellow facings for artillery. Distinguishing colors for the different arms would change several times in later years.

A single-breasted swallow-tail coat with high-standing collar was introduced in 1810. The coat was without facing, and silver lace about the buttonholes was its chief ornamentation. At the time, many people felt that fancy-colored uniforms too closely resembled the trappings of monarchies and had no place in an American Army. A civilian-type "stovepipe" hat, with a leather cockade on the side, was also a part of the uniform. Later it was succeeded by a stiff military cap with a high crown and plume, like that popular in European armies during that era. It was called a *shako.*

During the War of 1812 uniform regulations became more specific. For example, the exact number of inches a button was to be placed from the bottom of a coat was clearly stated. Colored facings continued to be forbidden. Blue uniforms were prescribed for all troops except rifle units, which wore a gray uniform. The standing collar of the coat was to reach the tip of the ear, and the coat was decorated with horizontal tape trim and blind buttonholes.

For dress, generals wore a cocked hat. This was a hat with a fairly high, stiff crown with the wide brim turned up on two sides and fastened to the crown. The commander in chief wore a white plume in his hat. Major generals wore a black-and-white plume. The inspector general and the adjutant general wore black, white and red. The quartermaster general wore a black plume. Other officers wore a chapeau. This was similar to the cocked hat but not nearly as large.

Infantry and cavalry officers wore silver epaulets at this time. All other officers, including generals, wore gold. The practice of wearing one or two epaulets according to rank was continued. General officers were privileged to wear shoes of any pattern, but the buckles must be of gold. Breeches gradually gave way to pantaloons. These were rather close-fitting garments which combined breeches and stockings. They extended from the waist to the instep and often were held down by a strap passing under the foot. Officers wore hussar boots, which came to the knee, decorated with gold tassels. Mounted troops wore a green coat with black collar, black lapels and black cuffs, white breeches, and high black boots. A stiff leather jockey-cap-type helmet was worn.

A shortage of blue cloth resulted in several substitutions of color during the War of 1812. Gray and brown makeshifts were common. These uniforms were ill-fitting and plain. Coatees and "roundabout" jack-

Bell-crown artillery cap with cap plate of the 3rd Artillery Regiment, circa 1821. Very few leather caps of this period have survived. This specimen gives an excellent idea of how this cap really looked. THE SMITHSONIAN INSTITUTION

25

Dragoon cap plate, 1833, consisting of a brass heraldic star upon which is superimposed a silvered brass eagle. Interestingly, the eagle is basically of the same Napoleonic pattern adopted by the British Army following the Battle of Waterloo, altered by omitting the lightning bolts in the talons and adding a wreath to the breast. THE SMITHSONIAN INSTITUTION

ets, short garments coming to the waist, were frequently worn. Short overalls with loose trousers coming to mid-calf also were issued in considerable quantities. A leather cylindrical shako with a high front appeared in 1813. It had a leather flap in the rear which could be let down to protect the back of the neck.

When quantities of a rough gray cloth became available, it was used to make uniforms for Brigadier General Winfield Scott's First Brigade of Regular Infantry. This brigade performed so gallantly at the Battle of Chippewa that its gray uniform became a kind of badge of honor, and the color was adopted for the cadet uniform at West Point. It was the origin of what since has come to be known as the "cadet gray" used for uniforms by the majority of military schools in this country.

Until this time the cadets of the United States Military Academy, which had been founded in 1802, wore the regular Army uniform. The first gray uniform consisted of a high-collared coat with tails, decorated with three rows of bright brass buttons down the front. The buttons were connected by double rows of black braid. Bright buttons and black braid also adorned the collar, lower sleeves and tails. Braid was worn, too, on the outside seams of the trouser legs. For summer white trousers were provided. These, oddly enough, had a row of bright brass buttons down the outside seam. A black leather shako and white cross belts were worn with the gray uniform. In many respects this uniform was like that worn at West Point today.

At the beginning of the second decade

of the nineteenth century, the large brass plate worn on the front of the cadet shako displayed a "trophy" of flags, swords, and muskets together with a United States shield. (A trophy is a collection of arms usually arranged about a shield, a helmet, or a breastplate. It originated as a sign of victory and valor and derives from the ancient Greek custom of displaying a defeated enemy's arms and armor on a tree or pole on the battlefield.) Over the trophy appeared an eagle holding thunderbolts and a laurel branch. At the top of the shako plate was a scroll bearing the words MILITARY ACADEMY.

The flaming shell, a spherical shell or bomb with tongues of flame spouting from the fuse hole — the identifying insignia of the Ordnance Corps — came into being about this time. Although the Ordnance Corps, responsible for the design and procurement of arms, was not founded until 1812, its insignia is the oldest in continuous use in the Army. The flaming shell is, indeed, probably the oldest military insignia in the world. It is based upon the small hand-thrown spherical shell with projecting fuse-hole collar which was an offensive weapon in the seventeenth century. It was sometimes called a *granado*, the Latin word for pomegranate, which it resembled in shape. From this stem the words "grenade" and "grenadier," — the soldier who threw the shell. After the spherical grenade ceased to be used, the name grenadier was retained to designate elite infantry troops. The term still is used with that meaning.

The insignia itself was first used in the United States Army as a general military ornament, without regard to any branch.

From 1821 to 1832, ordnance was merged with artillery and the flaming bomb was prescribed for those two branches alone. During the 1830's, there was an ordnance insignia of crossed cannon, with "U" on one side, "S" on the other, and a flaming shell above. Then, in 1851, the flaming shell was prescribed for ordnance alone and has been the exclusive insignia of that branch ever since.

In 1816, cadets at the United States Military Academy were issued a "common round hat." This was a stovepipe, high-crowned hat like that worn by civilians. It was decorated on the left side with a leather cockade bearing a small metal eagle. Later a tall, bell-crowned leather cap similar to that worn in the regular Army was adopted. It had a brass scale chin strap, a diamond-shaped front plate bearing an eagle, and a long worsted pompon on its top.

During 1816 members of the regular Army were ordered to wear a black cockade with a gilt eagle on their headpieces. They also were told that their coat collars should be as high as the lower tip of the ear but only "as high in front as the chin will permit in turning the head." Although not nearly as uncomfortable as the previous coat collar, it still forced the wearer to keep his chin up and face forward at all times.

Generals, corps artillery officers, and infantry officers all wore the chapeau, similar to the one worn in the War of 1812. Light artillery officers wore a heavy, round, stiff black hat with tassels falling from the top on the right side.

Light artillerymen wore a short coatee

27

Branch insignia of the Corps of Engineers. This turreted castle device was adopted in 1840. It was first used with an eagle above the castle as a cap device both for cadets at West Point and for the Engineers. Later the device was used by the Engineers alone and the eagle was omitted. Selection of the castle followed the first major construction project of the Corps of Engineers — the building of a system of castlelike fortifications protecting a series of Atlantic Coast harbors. These fortifications were, in fact, called castles. U. S. ARMY PHOTOGRAPH

of blue, riflemen a short gray coat. The rest of the Army wore long blue coats. Officers now wore the sash only while on duty instead of on all occasions, as in the past.

In 1821, the uniform regulations went to considerable length to describe the quality and pattern of the uniform. Blue was prescribed as the national uniform color. All officers above the rank of captain wore the *chapeau de bras*. This was a hat with a stiff brim turned up on two sides, flexible enough to be pressed together so that it could be easily carried under the arm — as contrasted to the ordinary chapeau, which was stiff and bulky. Captains, lieutenants, and enlisted personnel wore the high crown shako or "tar bucket." Officers' shakos were decorated with gold or silver braid while those of enlisted men had worsted braid. At the top front of the shako was a colored pompon in the color of the wearer's branch. Artillery wore yellow, light artillery red and white, infantry white, and rifle companies green.

During this period captains and lieutenants wore "wings" instead of shoulder straps and epaulets. These wings, worn on both shoulders regardless of rank, were ornamental pieces extending out over the shoulder seam of the coat. They were silver for infantry and gold for other branches.

Enlisted men at the time were issued laced shoes somewhat like those worn at present — except for one striking difference. They were the same for both feet, with no "left" or "right." Only after considerable wear did a shoe set to the foot. Captains and lieutenants wore short boots that came to the calf. Mounted officers wore high boots.

In 1825, captains, lieutenants, and enlisted men discarded the heavy clumsy tarbucket shako in favor of a lightweight cloth "yachting cap." Of soft cloth, it had a large visor and a large floppy crown. At about the same time an arc was added to the chevron of the adjutant and the sergeant major. Uniform facings in the colors of the different branches were reintroduced. Artillery wore yellow facings; light artillery, yellow and red; grenadiers, red; light infantry, white and red; infantry, white; rifles, green; dragoons, orange.

During 1832 officers were directed to wear knee-length, double-breasted coats and two epaulets, regardless of rank. General officers continued to be identified by the number of stars on the epaulet. The eagle insignia, to identify colonels, was introduced for the first time. Lieutenant colonels wore plain gold epaulets similar to those of generals and colonels. Majors had epaulets of gold and silver intertwined and without rank insignia. Captains wore smaller epaulets without rank insignia, silver for infantry and gold for other branches. Lieutenants wore still smaller epaulets in the same manner as captains. All officers except generals bore their regimental number on each epaulet.

Bands of music, other than fifes and drums, were first authorized in 1834. Band members drilled as regular soldiers and were liable for general duty if required. Apparently their duties as musicians were secondary.

The slightly curved shoulder strap worn across the shoulder at the top seam of the sleeve, similar to that on an officer's blue uniform today, was first authorized in 1836. Generals wore straps with gold-embroi-dered edge, their rank indicated by the number of stars within the edge. The commander in chief bore three stars, a major general, two, and a brigadier general, one Infantry officers wore a strap with silver-embroidered edge while officers' straps for other branches had a gold-embroidered edge. Colonels wore an eagle in the center of the strap, the eagle facing forward, while lieutenant colonels had an oak leaf at each end of the strap. These were the same color as the edging. Majors wore oak leaves in the same manner as lieutenant colonels, except that they were the opposite color from that of the edging. Captains had two bars at each end of the strap. These bars were the same color as the embroidered edge. First lieutenants wore a single bar in the same manner. Second lieutenants wore an embroidered-edged shoulder strap without a rank device of any kind. It would not be until well along in World War I that the lowly second lieutenant would be given distinctive rank insignia.

Staff officers wore *aiguillettes* on the undress coat at this time. These aiguillettes consisted of gold cord circling the left shoulder and hanging in loops across the chest. The hanging ends terminated in tapering metal points or "pencils."

The word aiguillette originally referred to the lacing used to fasten pieces of armor together. As usually is the case with military trappings of ancient origin, several fanciful tales have been told about the origin of the aiguillette. One has it that the decoration originated with a long cord and attached pencil used by staff officers to write messages. Another account ascribes the origin to an old custom of an aide-de-camp carrying a coiled rope with peg attached so that he could picket his general's horse. Another more fanciful tale is that after French troops had behaved badly in battle, some were singled out for hanging, as a lesson to the others. The troops asked for a chance to redeem themselves, saying they would wear a rope with spike attached around their shoulders so that they could be hanged immediately if they failed again. Supposedly they were forgiven and thereafter proved themselves such redoubtable fighters that the rope and spike became a badge of honor.

In 1836, crossed cannon were adopted as the insignia for the artillery. Two years later a Corps of Topographical Engineers was formed. These specialists engaged in surveying, heavy construction work, and reconnaissance. They also did considerable mapping and exploration.

Tall black beaver shakos resembling a section of stovepipe fitted with a flat visor were adopted in 1839 for the cadets at West Point. These had a tall worsted pompon in front. For a time the crossed cannon insignia of the artillery, with an eagle above, was worn as a front plate. For other than dress, a gray yachting-type cap like that worn by the members of the regular Army was prescribed as a forage cap.

The origin of the forage, or undress, cap goes back to the time when European soldiers lived off the land and searched or foraged for food when off duty. In order to save the regular duty uniform, a rough and comfortable uniform and cap were worn. It became known as a *forage* uniform.

A turreted castle was adopted in 1840 as the Engineer Corps insignia. It was first used in combination with an eagle as a cap device both for cadets at the United States Military Academy and members of the Engineer Corps. At that time the Military Academy was under the supervision and direction of the Chief of Engineers. Selection of a castle as the branch insignia followed the first major construction project of the newly formed Corps of Engineers. The project consisted of the building of a system of castlelike fortifications protecting Atlantic coast harbors.

Several uniform changes occurred during the Mexican War, 1846–1848. An attempt was made to provide a practical and comfortable campaign uniform in addition to the dress and general duty uniform. Unfortunately, however, the attempt failed and the troops had to fight in heavy uniforms ill adapted to the Mexican climate.

Chevrons of three stripes for sergeants and two for corporals were provided at this time. It was the first occasion when chevrons of more than one stripe were used to indicate rank. The chevrons were large, extending from seam to seam, and were worn point upward. In 1861, the points would be worn down and would remain that way until shortly before World War I when small chevrons with the point up were adopted. Chevrons were worn in the color of the branch of the wearer as follows: artillery, scarlet; infantry, light blue; rifles, green; cavalry, orange.

The embroidered edge or border of the shoulder straps of all officers was now gold regardless of branch of service. At the same time the leaf of the lieutenant colonel was prescribed as silver, and a gold leaf was prescribed for majors.

The size of military bands was increased in the mid-1840's. It was provided that bandsmen no longer would be mustered with the other troops but would be a separate unit on the headquarters staff. Bandsmen were assigned duties in time of war of acting as stretcher-bearers, messengers, and water-carriers. With the exception of water-carrying, these duties were performed by bandsmen on through World War II.

In 1850, the uniform of the Military Academy band was changed from white with red trimmings to dark blue with red trimmings. This uniform was worn throughout the Civil War period.

Crossed sabers with the edges up were first used as a distinguishing device for dragoons in 1850. Then, in 1855, two regiments of cavalry were raised, but not until three years later did they wear the saber insignia. In 1861, all mounted regiments were merged into cavalry and the crossed saber insignia was continued.

In 1853, a new dress cap was prescribed for the cadets at West Point. This was a cap with straight front and sides and a sharply sloping back, in the French tradition. Cadet officers' caps were decorated with a drooping plume of black cock feathers. Other cadets wore a tall black pompon. In 1855, a clumsy and uncomfortable shako, also of French pattern, was adopted. This monstrosity was decorated with cords, tassels, and pompon. Then, during the 1860's, the soft-sided, hard-top, French-influenced *kepi*, like that worn by members of the regular Army, was accepted as a forage cap.

This enlisted man's pompom eagle of 1851 was worn attached to the base of the pompom. It is similar to the eagle worn on the shako in the 1830's. Officers wore a similar design worked in a gold embroidery on cloth. THE SMITHSONIAN INSTITUTION

*General U. S. Grant and staff and line officers,
Civil War era. The officers in the foreground
are wearing the comfortable, rugged, and
popular black felt hat prescribed for both
officers and enlisted men.* U. S. SIGNAL CORPS

3

From the Civil War to the Spanish-American War

The uniform regulations of 1861 provided a dark blue, high-collared frock coat for both officers and enlisted foot soldiers. This was double-breasted for all officers above the rank of captain. Captains, lieutenants, and enlisted foot soldiers wore a single-breasted model.

General officers had a dark blue velvet collar and cuffs. Rank could be determined by the number and the placement of the coat buttons. Major generals had 2 rows of buttons down the front with nine buttons in each row, placed in sets of 3. Brigadier generals wore 8 buttons in each row, placed in pairs. Colonels, lieutenant colonels, and majors wore 7 equally spaced buttons in each row. Captains, lieutenants, and enlisted foot soldiers wore one row of 9 buttons.

The collar and the pointed cuffs of the enlisted man's coat were trimmed with colored braid according to the branch of service: artillery wore scarlet; infantry, sky

Infantry private in fatigue marching order, 1861. The dark blue, four-button fatigue jacket was worn for campaign duty. The "forage cap" is patterned after the French kepi. THE SMITHSONIAN INSTITUTION

Infantry private, 1861. Shown here is the "single-breasted frock coat of dark blue cloth" prescribed for all enlisted "foot" men. The diagonal "half chevron" on each lower sleeve indicates five years of faithful service. The light infantry bugle hat plate identifies the soldier as an infantryman. The "A" indicates Company A. The "1" indicates the 1st Infantry Regiment. THE SMITHSONIAN INSTITUTION

34

blue; engineers, yellow; ordnance and hospital stewards, crimson.

Cavalry and light artillery enlisted men wore a high-collared, waist-length, dark blue jacket with twelve buttons down the front. The jacket was decorated about the collar, down the front, and around the bottom with colored braid. This was scarlet for light artillery and yellow for cavalry.

Musicians wore either the long frock coat or the short jacket, depending upon whether they were serving with foot or mounted troops. Musicians' coats and jackets were decorated across the breast with rows of colored braid in the color of the wearer's branch.

For fatigue wear, enlisted men had a dark blue sack coat with four buttons down the front. It was a loose-fitting, comfortable garment.

Light artillery officers were provided with a short blue jacket trimmed in scarlet. This had gold "Russian" shoulder knots. The knots were twisted gold cords ending in a trefoil at the shoulder seam. Rank insignia was worn in the center of the knot.

General officers and ordnance officers wore dark blue trousers without a stripe on the outer seam. Officers of the general staff and of the staff corps wore a gold stripe one-eighth of an inch wide on each outside trouser seam. Other officers wore a one-eighth-inch-wide colored trouser stripe in the color of their branch. Medical cadets wore a similar stripe in buff color.

Enlisted men wore dark blue trousers. Corporals had a one-half-inch stripe and sergeants a one-and-one-half-inch trouser stripe in the color of their branch. Hospital stewards and ordnance sergeants

Infantry sergeant major, uniform regulations of 1861. THE SMITHSONIAN INSTITUTION

Light artillery corporal in the uniform of 1861. The coat is the "shell jacket" prescribed for cavalry and light artillery. THE SMITHSONIAN INSTITUTION

wore a one-and-one-half-inch trouser stripe of crimson.

A black felt hat with a crown much like an inverted flowerpot was prescribed for both officers and enlisted men. General officers wore a gold hat cord with acorn-shaped ends. Other officers had a gold and black silk hat cord with acorn ends. Enlisted men wore a worsted hat cord, also with acorn ends, in the color of their branch.

Generals wore a silver embroidered "U. S." within a gold embroidered wreath on a black velvet background as a hat device. Other officers had, as a hat device, a gold embroidered wreath within which was the insignia of their branch. The insignia now were as follows: engineers, a silver turreted castle: topographical engineers, a gold-embroidered shield; ordnance, a gold-embroidered flaming bomb; cavalry, gold-embroidered crossed sabers with the regimental number in silver above; artillery, gold-embroidered crossed cannon with the regimental number in silver above; infantry, a gold-embroidered bugle or hunting horn with the regiment number in silver inside the circle of the horn or bugle.

The early use of the bugle as infantry insignia, later to be replaced by crossed muskets and then by crossed rifles, stemmed from the fact that all rifle and light infantry troops in the late eighteenth and early nineteenth centuries were used chiefly as scouts or skirmishers ahead of the main body of troops. At that time orders were given in the field by the beat of a drum. Riflemen and light infantry, moving rapidly, found the drum too cumbersome and used instead, the bugle or hunting horn to sound orders.

36

Enlisted men wore the distinguishing insignia of their branch in brass on the front of the hat. Hospital stewards wore the Roman letters "U.S." in white metal.

The hats were decorated on the left side with feathers. Generals, colonels, lieutenant colonels and majors wore three feathers; captains and lieutenants, two; enlisted men, one. The right side of the hat had the brim turned up and secured to the crown by a metal eagle. All serving with regiments wore the regimental number in combination with the branch insignia. Enlisted men also wore the letter designating the company in which they served.

Light artillery units at this time continued to wear a shako decorated with a drooping red horsehair plume, cord, and tassels. On its front were crossed cannon and the regimental number, with an eagle above. For fatigue a *kepi* was worn. This actually was the French-type shako with soft sides which allowed the stiff top to fall forward to the visor.

Officers wore epaulets for dress. The major general commanding the army wore a large star on the pad of the epaulet and two smaller stars on the strap. These were of silver embroidery. Major generals wore the same, except that there was only one small star on the strap. Brigadier generals wore a single silver-embroidered star. The rank of colonels was indicated by a silver-embroidered eagle on the strap. Lieutenant colonels had a silver-embroidered leaf. Majors had a plain strap. The fringe on the epaulets of these officers, of dull and bright gold bullion, was three and one-half inches long and one half inch in diameter. Officers of lower rank wore similar epaulets, except that the fringe was only two and one-half

Artillery musician (drummer), 1861. His hat insignia identifies him as belonging to Company A, 1st Artillery Regiment. The coat is the same as that worn by all "foot" men except for the cloth lace on the breast, in the color of the wearer's branch. The color in this case is scarlet. THE SMITHSONIAN INSTITUTION

With his trousers tucked into the tops of his heavy socks, this young Union drummer boy is no recruiting-poster soldier. He is a veteran campaigner. This true-to-life drawing was made in the field at Beverly Ford, Virginia, on August 11, 1863. THE LIBRARY OF CONGRESS

inches long. For captains, it was one-fourth of an inch in diameter, for lieutenants, one-eighth inch. Captains wore two silver-embroidered bars on the strap of the epaulet. First lieutenants wore one. Second lieutenants had no rank device.

On the epaulet pad, topographical engineers wore a gold-embroidered shield with the letter "T" on one side and the letter "E" on the other. These were of silver metal. Engineer officers wore a silver metal turreted castle on the pad. Medical Staff officers had a gold-embroidered wreath; within it were the silver-embroidered letters "M.S." in Old English. Pay Department officers wore the same wreath but with the letters "P.D." in silver embroidery. Ordnance officers wore a silver-embroidered flaming shell.

Officers serving with regiments bore the number of the regiment embroidered in gold within a silver-embroidered circle upon a cloth background colored as follows: artillery, scarlet; infantry, light blue; cavalry, yellow.

Enlisted men wore brass shoulder scales on the dress coat. These were somewhat similar in general design to officers' epaulets but they were all metal and without fringe. They were a holdover from the days when metal protection was worn on the shoulders to ward off saber blows.

Officers wore shoulder straps with gold-embroidered edges across the shoulder seam of the fatigue coat. Since the usual straps with gold bullion edges and insignia were rather expensive, stamped brass and enameled substitutes often were used in the field.

The advent of the Civil War found this

country ill prepared to fight a conflict of any considerable size or duration. The small Regular Army had to be supplemented by state units. When sufficient volunteers did not come forward to serve, it was necessary to resort to conscription. The tremendous demands for food, clothing, and arms imposed problems that continued throughout the war. The state militia units and the many independent military organizations which first came forward to the aid of the Regular Army were, like their counterparts in the Revolutionary War, often colorfully uniformed and were trained and equipped in varying degrees of effectiveness.

Some of the state and independent outfits were uniformed very much like the Regular Army. Some wore gray uniforms much like those presently worn by the cadets at West Point. Of all the uniforms, none were more colorful than the Zouave outfits based upon the fancy uniform worn by the Algerian Zouaves of the French Army during the Crimean War. This uniform, as modified in America, usually consisted of a short, fancy, embroidery-decorated "monkey jacket," a fez (a tasseled cloth cap), loose baggy trousers, high-button shoes, and a broad cummerbund. The uniforms did not hold up well in rugged campaigning, and their bright colors made their wearers easy targets for enemy sharpshooters. Usually they were soon replaced by the more practical uniform of the regular infantryman.

During active campaigning Yankee soldiers generally wore what they pleased. The absurd kepi was extremely impractical for field soldiering. Far more practical was the black felt hat often called the "Jeff

This sketch of a youthful sergeant major of the 12th New York Volunteer Regiment was made at Stoneman's Switch, Virginia (near Fredericksburg), in January 1863. It pictures realistically the U.S. Army Civil War combat soldier. THE LIBRARY OF CONGRESS

39

In 1863, enlisted personnel operating the new electric telegraph system and those performing other signal duties were formed into a Signal Corps, and crossed signal flags were adopted as the distinctive device. In 1884 a vertical torch was added to the insignia, and the identifying device of the Signal Corps has remained unchanged ever since. U. S. ARMY PHOTOGRAPH

Davis" or "Kossuth" hat. It was adopted for the United States Army by Jefferson Davis while he was Secretary of War and was of the pattern worn by the Hungarian patriot Louis Kossuth when he toured the United States. Veteran soldiers were quick to appreciate its comfort and usefulness in keeping rain and sun off the face and back of the neck. Eventually it came to be identified with veteran outfits. Confederate troops were apt to be more careful in their tactics when they saw a number of black hats in the Union lines.

Mounted troops wore a sky blue overcoat with a so-called stand-and-fall collar. (Actually it was like a modern soft shirt collar in design.) Double-breasted, it had two rows of brass buttons down the front. The bottom of the coat reached six inches below the knees. A sky blue cape lined with cloth the color of the wearer's branch was attached under the coat collar. This cape, large and full, extended to the sleeve cuff. It caught the eye when the cape was thrown back over the shoulders and displayed the brightly colored lining. Foot troops wore a similar but shorter coat and cape.

Officers wore a dark blue overcoat and cape. The coat was closed by four black silk frogs on the front. (A frog is a fastening of braid woven into an ornamental loop design. A buttonlike device on one side fits through a loop on the other.) Rank was indicated on the sleeve by varying rows of braid.

Corps badges were introduced during the conflict. In the Civil War Army — by far the largest ever raised up to that time — there were 25 Army corps. Each had an identification badge. The badges usually were worn on the cap or hat, though sometimes officers wore them on the left breast. Commonly of cloth or enameled brass, the badges also could be purchased in enameled gold or silver if the soldiers wished to buy them.

There was a great variety of shapes and colors in the corps badges. For example, the First Corps was identified by a circle; the Second by a trefoil; the Third by a diamond; the Fourth by a triangle; the Fifth by a Maltese cross . . . and so on through a series of crescents, shields, arrows, and hearts. Furthermore, the badges were of different colors for the subordinate units within the corps. Thus the first division of any corps wore a red device; the second, white; the third, blue; the fourth, orange; the fifth, green. The various cavalry corps, the engineers, and the Signal Corps also had distinctive badges.

In 1863, the old Corps of Topographical Engineers was consolidated with the Corps of Engineers. In the same year the enlisted men operating the new telegraph system and those performing signal duties of various kinds were formed into a Signal Corps and wore crossed signal flags on their sleeves as an identifying device.

During the Civil War a limited number of civilian women nurses were hired for service in Army hospitals. Since these women had no official status, they could not be assigned to combat areas as readily as if they had been members of the military service.

Among the elite combat outfits of the Civil War were two regiments of sharpshooters which gained fame for prowess

Enlisted men's blue dress uniform of 1882. The chevrons and crossed signal flags on the upper sleeve identify this soldier as a Signal Corps sergeant. NATIONAL ARCHIVES

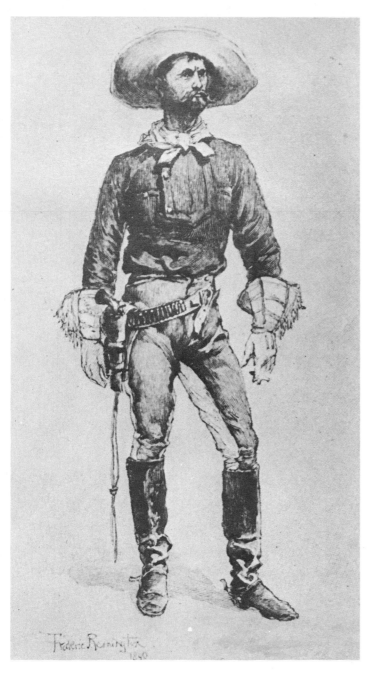

This Remington drawing shows a cavalry officer in campaign dress for duty against the Indians on the Western plains. His practical uniform is intended to provide maximum utility and comfort. NATIONAL ARCHIVES

with rifles. They were clothed in a distinctive green uniform. On the kepi, officers wore a crossed rifle insignia with the letters "US" above and "SS" below, in Old English, all enclosed within a wreath. Enlisted men wore the same insignia without the wreath. It was not the first time that the Army had worn green uniforms. The Corps of Artificiers of 1812–1815, attached to the Quartermaster General's Department, had been uniformed in green coats with red collars and green pantaloons.

During the Civil War, military bands achieved a higher quality, chiefly because many of the state militia bands mustered into Federal service were crack musical organizations. They were up front as often as in the rear. The casualty rate among bandsmen was very high.

When the administration of the United States Military Academy was taken from the Engineer Corps in 1869, the engineer insignia was removed from the cadet cap. In its place was a sunburst with a shield bearing the insignia of engineers, artillery, infantry and cavalry on its center. The cap, though still in the French tradition, was not as high in the crown as previously.

Following the Civil War, the Army once again was drastically reduced in size. It still had an important job, however, in the wars against the Western Indian tribes. The small western army was a tough, professional outfit. It had to be in order to survive.

This hard-riding, hard-marching, hard-fighting army has been pictured in neatly tailored uniforms in many motion pictures and on television. But an artist such as

Frederic Remington was one of the most famous artists of the Old West. He realistically depicted his subjects as he actually saw them. Shown here is his drawing of a cavalry bugler in dress uniform during the Indian troubles which followed the Civil War. NATIONAL ARCHIVES

43

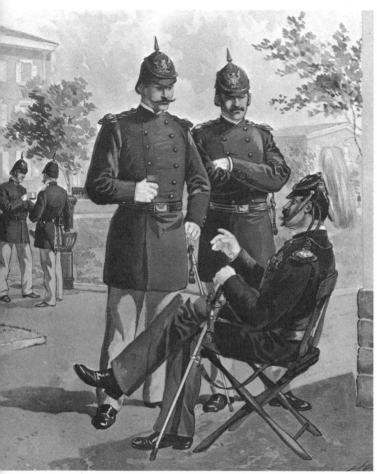

Officers and enlisted men, 1880-1885. U. S.
ARMY PHOTOGRAPH

Frederic Remington, who lived with the army, portrayed it more accurately. His paintings reveal that the soldier of the frontier was not like a figure on an Army recruiting poster.

In many respects, the officially prescribed uniform, a holdover from the Civil War, was ill adapted to campaigning on the western plains. Although the short jacket was comfortable in cold and even in fairly moderate weather, it was almost unbearable to a soldier riding or marching under a blazing sun. Despite what one has seen on the television screen, blue shirts were *not* worn by enlisted men until the 1880's. Up until that time the enlisted man sweated out his western duty in a gray flannel shirt and heavy blue jacket. It is true, however, that some officers availed themselves earlier of the comfort of the light blue shirt.

Cavalrymen wore high boots. Dismounted soldiers usually wore shoes with leggings. Generally, however, they discarded the hot leggings and tucked their trouser legs into the tops of their long, heavy socks — a custom begun during the Civil War. Though not military-looking, it was comfortable and practical when tramping miles through sand and sagebrush.

General officers have long been privileged, within limits, to design their own uniforms. Despite this freedom, generals usually have been conservative in their uniforms. For example, independent-minded George Patton had only a fancy belt buckle and a couple of nonregulation revolvers. Douglas MacArthur, another independent general, merely added a band of gold-embroidered leaves and acorns about his cap.

Uniform for officers and enlisted men, 1872-1881. All personnel wore dark blue coats. With the exception of general officers, who wore dark blue trousers, all personnel wore sky blue trousers. Commissioned and noncommissioned officers wore trousers stripes of the color of their branch. U. S. ARMY PHOTOGRAPH

Cavalry and infantry enlisted men, dress and full dress uniforms, 1888. The mounted cavalrymen wear full dress uniforms with gold or yellow braid across the front and the Prussian-influenced helmet with fall-yellow plume. The infantrymen wear the dress uniform with spiked helmet. These German-influenced uniforms never suited the American fighting men. NATIONAL ARCHIVES

It was not so, however, of George Armstrong Custer, the youthful cavalry general who lost most of his regiment and his own life at the Battle of the Little Big Horn. Custer favored a double-breasted black *velvet* jacket with loops of gold braid extending well above the elbows. His shirt, which had a wide sailor collar decorated with a star at each corner, was turned down over his coat collar. He wore a brilliant red tie and an extremely broad-brimmed hat with a cord of gold braid and a large star pinned to its front.

When the tiny kingdom of Prussia drubbed the French military giant in 1870, Prussian military styles became popular. The United States followed the rush to imitate Prussian uniforms. Within two years after the end of the Franco-Prussian War, the United States Army was outfitted in slashed cuffs and coat skirts and a hard felt spiked helmet. Officers and mounted troops wore a drooping plume the color of their branch in place of the spike. Somehow this outfit did not become the American fighting man.

Several other changes in uniform occurred in 1872. General officers, colonels, lieutenant colonels and majors wore a double-breasted coat. Captains and lieutenants abandoned their single-breasted pattern for the double-breasted model, which had two rows of nine buttons each down the breast. For a time officers wore gold lace trim on the coat cuffs in the German manner, but this decoration lasted only briefly.

At this time generals and staff officers wore dark blue trousers without a leg stripe. Other officers, except infantry, wore light blue trousers with a one-and-one-half-inch

*Officers and cadets of the U. S.
Military Academy, West Point, 1888.* U. S.
ARMY PHOTOGRAPH

Officers and enlisted men, 1888, wearing overcoats and capes. U. S. ARMY PHOTOGRAPH

stripe in the color of their branch. Infantry officers wore a dark blue stripe.

At the beginning of the Revolutionary War each colony had its own plans for providing chaplains. The legal origin for the United States Army's Corps of Chaplains is found in a resolution of the Continental Congress dated July 29, 1775 which provided that chaplains be paid the same pay as that allowed for captains. By the end of the Revolution, a fairly well-developed organization of chaplains had evolved. Their increasing importance is indicated by the fact that their monthly pay became that of a colonel.

Details of the uniforms of the early chaplains are very meager but it appears that until 1825 they wore a uniform similar to that of dismounted officers.

Until the Civil War there were very few chaplains in the military service, and these few had to perform additional duties as schoolmasters and librarians. Then, during the Civil War, the chaplaincy received marked support. During this war many chaplains wore a plain black coat and trousers and an officer's black hat or dark blue kepi. A silver "U.S." within a gold wreath was worn on the front of the hat or cap. Some chaplains, especially those serving with state militia units, liked fancier garb and were allowed to wear it. There are pictures of Civil War chaplains wearing elaborate uniforms which differ little from those worn by regimental officers.

In 1880, chaplains began wearing black velvet shoulder straps with a gold-embroidered shepherd's crook insignia. In 1899, this insignia was replaced by a Latin cross. The six-pointed Star of David and the two

Enlisted men, 1896-1907. The two figures in the foreground are wearing the general service uniform. The two figures in the left back- *ground are wearing variations of the work, or fatigue, uniform.* U. S. ARMY PHOTOGRAPH

Tablets of the Law as insignia for chaplains of the Jewish faith was introduced in 1908 when the first Jewish chaplains were appointed.

Over the years the official status of Army chaplains has improved greatly. During the Civil War they achieved the rank of captain. In 1904, legislation provided various grades of chaplains from first lieutenant to major. In 1920, the top rank was raised to lieutenant colonel, and in 1935 to colonel. In 1941, provision was made for appointment as high as brigadier general. Finally, in 1944, major general was designated as the senior chaplain rank.

Technically, a chaplain has rank without command — with rare exceptions. Today the chaplain, with his distinctive corps insignia, wears the same uniform as other officers.

The Army's first adjutant general was appointed on June 17, 1775, but it was not until 1872 that an insignia was adopted for what had become the Adjutant General's Department (now the Adjutant General's Corps). This insignia consists of a shield edged in gold with a blue field across the top. In the center of the field is a large white star with 6 white stars grouped on each side. Under the blue field are 7 white and 6 vertical red stripes.

In 1873, the West Point Band was provided with a blue uniform which, with a few modifications, is the same as that worn today. Five years later a new West Point cadet cap insignia was adopted. It consisted of a brass plate bearing the letters "USMA" along with an eagle and a crossed sword and pen.

In 1884, the crossed signal flags device worn on the coat sleeve by Signal Corps enlisted men was combined with a vertical torch to create the insignia for all Signal Corpsmen. Around the same time enlisted men began wearing a dark blue coat with a much shorter skirt. Trimmed in the color of the wearer's branch, it had a color patch on each side of the stand-up collar. This patch bore the regimental number or the corps device in brass. At the cuff of each sleeve was a colored vertical cloth strip. The skirts of the coat were slashed and faced with colored cloth. The coat was single-breasted, with nine buttons down the front. Colored shoulder straps, similar to the cloth shoulder straps extending from shoulder to collar, completed the garment. Sergeants wore a one-inch and corporals a half-inch colored trouser stripe on their sky blue trousers.

For undress, officers wore a single-breasted dark blue sack coat with five buttons down the breast. Black braid decorated the area of the buttons and the buttonholes, extending back on each side to terminate in frogs or fancy loops. Knots of black braid decorated the coat cuffs.

In the mid-1880's, white became the prescribed color for infantry — as it still is. Previously, in 1875, crossed rifles became the infantry insignia to replace the traditional light infantry bugle. For a time the crossed rifle insignia was modified to reflect each change in rifles adopted by the Army. But the practice was abandoned in 1924 when it was decided to use permanently the pattern of the musket fired by American troops in the Revolution.

In the 1880's, too, a loose ulster overcoat with an attached hood was introduced for officers. Orders also were issued that "in extreme southern latitudes" officers could wear straw hats similar to the flat-top straw "sailor" worn by civilians. This probably was the most unmilitary headgear that the United States Army ever authorized.

About the same time all officers except generals gave up wearing the sash.

Another new headgear appeared in 1885 — the wide-brimmed olive drab felt campaign hat, creased fore and aft. In somewhat modified form, it would be worn until World War II. A straight side cap, much like that worn by railroad conductors, was introduced in 1889. First worn only by officers, it later would be prescribed for enlisted men. In modified form it still is worn today. At the same time laced canvas leggings were issued for the first time.

Although the duties and the responsibilities of the Inspector General date from 1777, and an Inspector General's Department was created in 1818, an insignia was not adopted until 1890. It consists of a sword crossed with *fasces* (an ax in a bundle of rods). The sword represents the military establishment, and the fasces represents authority, fasces being the symbol of the ancient Roman magistrates. Superimposed on this device is a wreath bearing the motto DROIT ET AVANT (Right and Forward).

The quartermaster insignia was adopted in 1896 and has been retained since despite changes in organization and responsibilities of this branch. It consists of a spoked wheel with stars about the rim. A sword crossed with a key are superimposed on the

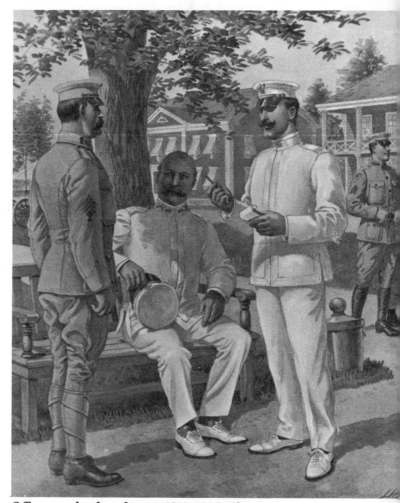

Officers and enlisted men, 1898-1907. The two officers are wearing white cotton uniforms. The enlisted men are wearing cotton khaki.
U. S. ARMY PHOTOGRAPH

Dress uniforms of noncommissioned officers, 1898-1907. U. S. ARMY PHOTOGRAPH

wheel. The sword represents the military character of the corps; the key and the wheel represent transportation and supply duties. An eagle with spread wings perches atop the wheel.

By the time the United States became involved in the Spanish-American War in 1898, the Army was planning to introduce a khaki field uniform. The word *khaki* is from the Persian and means "dust color." The uniform was first worn by British troops during the Indian Mutiny in 1857. In their regular white uniforms the British proved to be easy targets. Then a resourceful soldier discovered that the uniform could be made less conspicuous by dyeing it in coffee, curry powder, or mulberry juice — or even by soaking it in muddy water. The British, pleased by the discovery, later officially adopted the khaki uniform.

Though a few soldiers obtained khaki breeches during the war with Spain, khaki did not become an item of general issue in the United States Army until the war was over. Most American soldiers in the war were issued heavy blue trousers, canvas leggings, a heavy blue flannel shirt, and a wide-brimmed campaign hat. It was a hot and uncomfortable outfit to wear in Cuba.

The khaki uniform which was worn immediately following the Spanish-American War was similar for both officers and enlisted men. The coat was a five-button, single-breasted model with a stand-up collar which turned down on the outside. It had four outside patch pockets, each closed with a flap and button. Officers wore a cloth shoulder strap from the collar to the shoulder seam. This strap was in the color of their branch and had rank insignia at the outer end. Enlisted men wore a similar shoulder strap. In a few instances enlisted men also wore colored pocket flaps. Although white was now the prescribed color for infantry, some militia outfits still wore the old infantry blue. Khaki breeches were worn with this coat, together with laced canvas leggings for enlisted men and leather leggings or boots for officers.

For a short time a khaki-covered, high-crowned sun helmet was provided, but it never was popular and never replaced the felt campaign hat.

In the Spanish-American War the War Department officially recognized the need for women nurses and hired them in a civilian capacity at $30 a month. A widespread epidemic of typhoid fever in the camps and the inability of the service to enlist enough qualified men to do hospital duty forced the decision on the Army. About 1,000 nurses served in Cuba, Puerto Rico, the Philippines, aboard army transports, and in military hospitals at home. Their uniform was the customary white worn by nurses on duty.

The first West Point cadet field uniform was introduced in 1898. It consisted of a gray shirt, wide black tie, gray trousers with black stripes tucked into high, laced canvas leggings, an olive drab felt campaign hat creased fore and aft, and black shoes. Later the hat was blocked in the "Montana peak" style of the Regular Army.

During the same year the present United States Military Academy insignia was adopted and worn as a cap device. It consists of a United States shield upon which the helmet of Pallas Athene, Grecian god-

Winter uniforms, officers and enlisted men, 1898-1907. U. S. ARMY PHOTOGRAPH

*Khaki field uniform for enlisted men, 1898-
1900. The shoulder straps and chevrons are in
the color of the wearer's branch.* U. S. SIGNAL
CORPS

*Khaki field uniform for officers, 1898-1900.
Note that the shoulder straps are in the color
of the wearer's branch of service. The mounted
officers wear the khaki sun helmet, which was
used for only a short period.* U. S. ARMY
PHOTOGRAPH

dess of wisdom and the arts and trades, and a Grecian sword are superimposed. Perched on the top of the shield is an eagle with outstretched wings and a ribbonlike scroll bearing the words ·DUTY, HONOR, COUNTRY. In 1899, the "tar bucket" dress shako, similar to that worn today, was introduced for both the cadets and the members of the Army Band stationed at West Point.

Officers wearing winter uniforms with overcoats (and cape), 1898-1907. U. S. ARMY PHOTOGRAPH

Cadets, U. S. Military Academy, West Point, 1898-1907. In the left background are a cadet private in campaign uniform and a cadet corporal in dress uniform. The first figure in the foreground is a cadet first sergeant in full dress. The center figure is a cadet captain in full dress. The third figure in the foreground is a cadet adjutant, also in full dress. In the right background are a cadet private in full dress with white trousers and an infantry captain in full dress. The full dress uniforms worn by West Point cadets today are very similar to those worn during the period shown above.

U. S. SIGNAL CORPS

*Major general, general officers of the line and
staff corps, evening dress and mess jacket,
1902-1907.* NATIONAL ARCHIVES

4

From 1900 to 1920

The period between 1900 and 1917, or roughly from the end of the Spanish-American War to the beginning of World War I, saw the final flowering of Army uniforms in all their glory. During this era officers had uniforms for full dress, dress, service dress, and mess dress. Enlisted men had dress and service uniforms.

For full dress, officers wore a dark blue double-breasted frock coat with stand-up collar. Generals' collars were ornamented all around with gold-embroidered leaves. Gold epaulets with stars on the strap indicated their rank. On the pad was the arms of the United States. Coat cuffs were of velvet, with a decorative motif of gold-embroidered leaves. Rank was indicated on the sleeve cuff by stars. Other officers had a gold embroidered band about the top and bottom of the collar with silk the color of the wearer's branch between. Officers other than generals wore shoulder knots of braided gold wire instead of epaulets.

Rank of the officers was indicated by gold lace knots on the lower sleeve. These decorative knots appeared above a sleeve stripe of one-half-inch gold lace. The knot was composed of one large vertical loop with a smaller horizontal loop on each side at the bottom. The colonel's knot was of 5 strands of gold braid; the lieutenant colo-

Field and company grade infantry officers, full dress, 1902-1907. NATIONAL ARCHIVES

nel's of 4; the major's of 3; the captain's of 2; and the first lieutenant's of 1. The second lieutenant wore the sleeve stripe without the knots. Insignia indicating the wearer's branch was worn in the angle formed where the knots joined, except for second lieutenants, who wore their insignia midway of the width of the sleeve just above the stripe.

On the overcoat, rank was indicated in the same manner in black mohair braid. Generals wore two wide black mohair stripes with the stars of their rank between the stripes.

For full dress, general officers wore dark blue trousers with two one-half-inch gold stripes spaced one-fourth of an inch apart. Staff officers wore a single seven-eighths-inch gold trouser stripe on dark blue trousers. Engineer officers also wore dark blue trousers with a one-and-one-half-inch scarlet stripe piped in white. Other officers wore light blue trousers with a one-and-one-half-inch stripe in the color of their branch.

For dress, general officers wore a double-breasted dark blue sack coat with 2 rows of gilt buttons down the front. Generals wore 2 rows of 12 buttons each, arranged in groups of 4. Lieutenant generals wore 10 buttons in each row arranged in 3 groups. The upper and lower groups had 3 buttons each, and the center group had 4. Major generals wore 9 buttons in each row arranged in groups of 3. Brigadier generals wore 8 in each row arranged in groups of 2. If a general was the head of a branch of the service, he wore his branch insignia on his collar.

All other officers, for dress, wore a single-breasted coat of dark blue closed by buttons concealed under a flap. The coat was trimmed about the collar, down the front, around the bottom, and on the vertical side openings with lustrous black mohair braid one and one-half inches wide. Branch insignia was worn on each side of the collar.

Shoulder straps with raised gold-embroidered edges enclosed a rectangle the color of the branch, except for general officers, whose color was dark blue. Rank insignia of generals and colonels was embroidered in the center of the strap. For other officers, except second lieutenants, rank insignia was embroidered at each end of the strap. Second lieutenants wore a strap without rank insignia. Trousers were the same for dress as for full dress.

The service coat, single-breasted, olive drab, with standing collar, was closed by five bronze buttons. Rank insignia was worn at the shoulder seam of the cloth shoulder straps, which extended to the base of the collar where they were attached by a small bronze button. Small bronze buttons closed the flaps of each of the four outside patch pockets. General officers wore a one-half-inch stripe of black mohair braid around the cuff of the sleeve. All other officers wore a similar stripe of brown braid. Olive drab breeches and leather leggings or boots were worn with this uniform.

The full dress cap for general officers was dark blue with a bell crown similar to that presently worn. On the front, embroidered in gold, was the arms of the United States. The cap band was decorated with gold-embroidered leaves, as was the visor. Other officers wore a similar cap with a band of silk in the color of the wearer's branch and a gold stripe about the top and

Major general, officers of the staff corps and departments, general staff and line, dress uniform, 1902-1907. This is one of the famous Ogden prints. NATIONAL ARCHIVES

Uniforms of the World War I era. The campaign, or field, hat with the so-called Montana peak was worn only in this country. Overseas the "overseas" cap or steel helmet were worn. U. S. ARMY PHOTOGRAPH

bottom of the silk band. Colonels, lieutenant colonels, and majors wore embroidered gold oak leaves on the cap visor. The caps of captains and lieutenants had a plain patent-leather visor.

A special evening dress uniform was provided during this period. The dark blue coat was patterned closely after the "long tail" full dress coat worn by civilians. It was fitted with gilt buttons and the sleeves were decorated in the same manner as the full dress coat. Trousers were dark blue for cavalry, artillery and infantry. All other officers wore full dress trousers. A white stiff-bosomed full dress shirt with wing collar and black bow tie, white waistcoat, black shoes and socks, and full dress cap completed the outfit.

The blue mess uniform consisted of a short dark blue mess jacket reaching to the waist with lapels faced in the color of the wearer's branch. Sleeves were decorated in the same manner as the full dress coat. Full dress trousers were worn. A white or dark blue waistcoat, white stiff-bosomed dress shirt, wing collar, black bow tie, black shoes and socks, and full dress cap were worn.

The white mess uniform was similar, except that everything but the bow tie was white; even the sleeve decoration was of white braid.

A white uniform also was prescribed. This consisted of a white sack coat of the same pattern as the dress blue coat but trimmed with white braid. White cloth shoulder straps extended from the shoulder to the collar. White cap, white trousers, and white shoes and hose were worn with the uniform.

Uniforms for U. S. Army nurses and American Red Cross workers. The latter are identified by the cross on the front of the hat band.
U. S. ARMY PHOTOGRAPH

63

The service cap worn at the time was similar to that of today except that the bell crown was not as pronounced and the visor was shorter. The leather chin strap was secured on each side by a small bronze button. The arms of the United States in bronze appeared on the front of the cap.

By this time the so-called Montana peak campaign hat of olive drab felt was being worn. It was so named because the crown, dented on four sides, resembled a mountain peak. With this hat, general officers wore a double hat cord of gold bullion with acorns at the ends. Other commissioned officers wore a simliar cord of gold bullion intermixed with black silk thread and with gold and black acorns. Warrant officers (then designated army field clerks and field clerks Quartermaster Corps) ranked between commissioned officers and noncommissioned officers and wore hat cords of silver intertwined with black and with silver and black acorns.

For dress, enlisted men wore a dark blue single-breasted coat with standing collar and six gilt buttons down the front. It was trimmed about the collar and shoulder straps in the branch color. A decorative breast cord of the same color, attached to the left shoulder, passed around the collar and under the right arm, then back across the breast to the left shoulder where it terminated in hanging knots. A brass "U.S." and the insignia of the wearer's branch appeared on each side of the collar.

Many noncommissioned officers wore devices indicating their specialities. For example, lightning bolts identified electrical specialists and crossed batons denoted a drum major. The increasing technical character of the Army was reflected in many of the new ratings, such as ordnance sergeant, master signal electrician, sergeant of field music, master gunner, assistant engineer, radio sergeant, and chief mechanic.

The dress trousers of sergeants had an outside seam stripe one and one-fourth inches wide in the color of the branch. Corporals had a similar stripe one-half inch wide. Dress trousers for all enlisted men were light blue.

The dress cap was dark blue and had a welt the color of the branch about the top and bottom of the band. As a cap device, enlisted men wore the insignia of their branch with the number of their unit.

The winter service uniform coat for enlisted men consisted of a single-breasted, wool, olive drab sack coat with five dull bronze buttons down the front. The four outside patch pockets were each closed by a flap and a small, dull bronze button. The letters "U.S." and the branch insignia in dull bronze were worn on each side of the standing collar. Wool olive drab breeches were prescribed. Unmounted troops wore khaki canvas leggings. Mounted troops wore brown leather leggings. The belt was of brown leather with a square brass buckle.

The service cap was similar to that worn by officers. It had the branch insignia on the front in dull bronze. The service hat also was like the olive drab felt Montana peak hat worn by officers. A hat cord in the color of the branch was worn. This terminated in two acorns.

Coast artillery, manning the large fixed fortress guns and the big mobile railway guns defending the coast, now was identified by crossed cannon with a red-enam-

The American Soldier, 1781. PAINTING BY
H. CHARLES MC BARRON, FROM THE U. S. ARMY'S
"THE AMERICAN SOLDIER" SERIES

The troops in this painting wear the uniforms prescribed in the regulations of 1779 and supplied at the time of the Yorktown campaign — blue coats with distinctive facings for the infantry regiments from four groups of states: New England; New York and New Jersey; Pennsylvania, Delaware, Maryland and Virginia; and the Carolinas and Georgia. All of the infantry coats are lined with white and have white buttons. All the troops wear white "overalls" and waistcoats.

A lieutenant in the right foreground is recognizable by the epaulet on his left shoulder. He is in the uniform worn by the troops from New York and New Jersey, blue faced with buff. On his cocked hat he wears the black and red "Union" cockade introduced by General Washington in July 1780,

emblematic of the union of the American and French armies. He holds a spontoon, the weapon carried by all junior officers and sergeants in addition to their swords.

To the left of the lieutenant stands a private of the artillery in the blue coat faced with red and lined with red, trimmed with the yellow of artillery.

In the background, from left to right, are the New England troops from New Hampshire, Massachusetts, Rhode Island, and Connecticut, in blue faced with white, and a drummer in the colors reversed (behind the spontoon). Then come musicians in red faced with blue, the reversed colors of the units from Pennsylvania, Delaware, Maryland, and Virginia. At the far right are two field-grade officers from these same states in blue coats faced with red, with epaulets on both shoulders; the one on horseback wears a gorget, an officer's insignia worn in most European armies of the period.

U. S. ARMY PHOTOGRAPH

The American soldier, 1786. PAINTING BY
H. CHARLES MCBARRON, FROM THE U. S. ARMY'S
"THE AMERICAN SOLDIER" SERIES

In the fall of 1784 the entire U. S. Army consisted of eight infantry and two artillery companies. Four states — Connecticut, New York, New Jersey and Pennsylvania — were called on to furnish troops. Only New Jersey and Pennsylvania responded. The Army's missions were to occupy the forts along the frontier and protect the U. S. commissioners who were making treaties with the Indians. The uniform, adopted by the Secretary of War and approved by General George Washington in December, 1782, consisted of a blue coat with red facings, white lining and buttons for infantry, and red lining and yellow buttons for artillery. In the left foreground is a captain of artillery, an epaulet on his right shoulder, wearing the red-lined coat with yellow buttons. In the right foreground is an infantry private in the "fatigue vest made of blue cloth with a red cape and lineage" used for daily duties to spare the uniform coats. At times these fatigue vests were made by company tailors (as is the one shown); sometimes they were made merely by cutting down an old uniform coat, in which case they might retain the red cuffs. In the background is a field-grade officer, distinguished by his silver epaulets, inspecting a detachment of infantrymen in blue coats faced with red and lined with white. The infantrymen are headed by their musicians, uniformed in reversed colors, i.e., red coats with blue facings. The Army of 1784 was not always able to furnish uniforms even for the small number of troops in the service. The New Jersey detachment in 1784, for example, was issued blue coats with white facings, the old uniform of the New England line. The detachment's captain was forced to drop the men's rum ration in order to use the money to buy red cloth so that the company tailor could make all the coats alike. U. S. ARMY PHOTOGRAPH

The American soldier, 1794. PAINTING BY H.
CHARLES MC BARRON, FROM THE U.S. ARMY'S
"THE AMERICAN SOLDIER" SERIES

*The Army that on August 20, 1794, at the
Battle of Fallen Timbers avenged the defeats
suffered at the hands of the Indians in 1790
and 1791 was the creation of Major General
Anthony Wayne. Wayne insisted on rigid
discipline and strict training. Conscious of the
welfare of his men, he saw to it that supplies
were adequate and equipment satisfactory.
The Army at this time had been reorganized
into a "legion," a term widely used during the
eighteenth century to mean a composite
organization of all combat branches under a
single command. The Army, instead of being
composed of regiments, was made up of four
sub-legions, each commanded by a brigadier
general and each consisting of two infantry
battalions, one battalion of riflemen, one troop
of dragoons, and one company of artillery. To
develop* esprit de corps, *Wayne had each sub-
legion wear distinctive insignia. General
Wayne, in the left foreground, is wearing the
general officer's uniform of blue coat faced and
lined with buff, and the buff vest and breeches
worn during the Revolutionary War. He has
the two silver stars of a major general on his
gold epaulets. To the left rear of the general is
a dragoon orderly in his bearskin-crested
leather cap with red turban, denoting that he
is a member of the Second Sub-Legion. The
orderly's blue uniform faced with red and
lined with white, and white vest and breeches,
were established for all cavalry and infantry in
1782. In the right foreground is an infantry
junior officer identified by an epaulet on his
left shoulder and by his unbound bearskin-
crested hat. The colors of his uniform are the
same as that of the dragoon. In the background, men of the First Sub-Legion, identified
by the white binding and black bearskin crests
on their hats, advance under the command of
a captain armed with a spontoon.* U. S. ARMY
PHOTOGRAPH

The American soldier, 1805. PAINTING BY
H. CHARLES MCBARRON, FROM THE U. S. ARMY'S
"THE AMERICAN SOLDIER" SERIES

Following the Revolutionary War the U. S. Army had few trained technicians, particularly engineers, and had to depend greatly on foreign experts. To correct this situation the engineers were separated from the artillery branch and the Corps of Engineers, consisting of ten artillery and engineer cadets and seven engineer officers, was created in 1802. This Corps was to be stationed at West Point and was to constitute the Military Academy. In 1803 nineteen enlisted men were added to the Corps "to aid in making experiments and for other purposes." In the left foreground of this scene showing construction work near West Point in 1805 is an artillery cadet wearing the combination of commissioned-officer uniforms prescribed for cadets of artillery. His blue coat is faced and lined with red. It has yellow· buttons and wings piped with red — the coat
worn by artillery noncommissioned officers. On the left shoulder he wears the small epaulet prescribed for cadets. His officer's cocked hat bears the black national cockade with an eagle button and the red plume of the artillery. With his enlisted man's white linen summer "overalls" he is wearing officer's half-boots.

On the right of the scene is a engineer private in the blue coat with black velvet collar and cuffs and false yellow buttonholes on the collar, cuffs, and breast, adopted for the enlisted men of the Corps of Engineers in 1803. He is wearing white winter "overalls" and an artilleryman's cocked hat with a red plume. In the background, enlisted infantrymen are working, clad in the "coarse linen frock and fatigue trousers" prescribed by Congress as a part of the annual clothing allowance in March, 1802. For protection from the weather, old-issue hats, bandannas, and similar items were worn as headdress. U. S.
ARMY PHOTOGRAPH

The American soldier, 1812. PAINTING BY
H. CHARLES MC BARRON, FROM THE U. S. ARMY'S
"THE AMERICAN SOLDIER" SERIES

The Regiment of Light Artillery, an elite horse artillery corps, was raised in 1808 in response to President Thomas Jefferson's request for augmentation of the U. S. Army in the face of hostile British and French acts against the United States. Within four years it ranked first among all U. S. Army units. The regiment retained its position until disbanded in 1821.

Because of the growth of the Army during the War of 1812, several staff departments were organized to serve the troops in the field. One of these new organizations was the Hospital Department.

The figure on foot in the right foreground is a light artillery sergeant in the all-blue uniform trimmed with yellow prescribed in January, 1812, when the light artillery became the first organization of the Army to do away with colored facings. The rank is recognizable by
the yellow silk epaulets and the red sash. The sergeant wears a "yeoman crowned" shako, i.e., a shako wider at the top than at the bottom. It is trimmed with yellow cords, a yellow shako plate, and a red and white plume peculiar to the light artillery at this time.

The horseman in the foreground is an infantry surgeon in the uniform adopted in January, 1812. He may be identified by the silver embroidered collar on his plain blue coat, by the black ostrich feather in his black-bordered hat, and by the fact that he is not wearing epaulets. Behind the infantry surgeon and partially obscured by him is a gun with its mounted crew preceded by a caisson.

To the left in the background is a captain of light artillery in a blue coat with white breeches, with one gold epaulet on his right shoulder and three bars in the corner of his red, gold-laced saddlecloth. To his left is a trumpeter of light artillery in a coat of red, the reversed colors of the regimental uniform.
U. S. ARMY PHOTOGRAPH

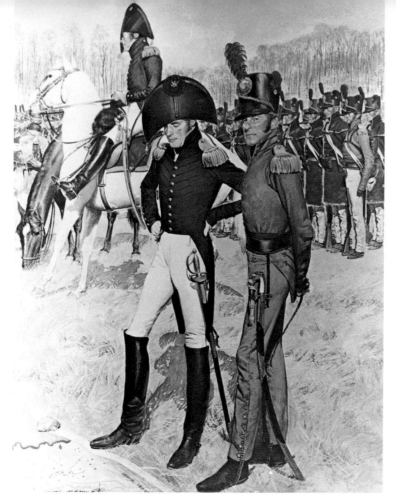

The American soldier, 1814. PAINTING BY
H. CHARLES MCBARRON, FROM THE U. S. ARMY'S
"THE AMERICAN SOLDIER" SERIES

*The War of 1812 was the cradle of the U.S.
Army's general staff. Staff departments and
staff procedures comparable to the best
available in European armies were developed.*

*In the scene shown here a general staff
officer stands in the left foreground in the
single-breasted blue coat with black herring-
bone false buttonholes on chest and cuffs, and
gold bullet buttons. The uniform was adopted
in 1813 and was worn for about twenty years.
Behind this officer is a mounted general officer.
His saddle, with its bearskin-covered pistol
holsters, rests on a blue saddlecloth with a
wide gold-lace border prescribed for general
and staff officers.*

In the right foreground is a rifle field-grade

*officer in the gray dress uniform adopted for
the rifle regiments in March, 1814. This
uniform was also worn later by the 26th
Infantry Regiment. The officer's shako is of the
same shape worn by the light artillery, but
with the distinctive round rifle regiment cap
plate and the green plume worn by rifle outfits.*

*A detachment of riflemen in their fringed
green summer linen rifle frocks, the only
remains of the green uniform formerly worn
by the rifle regiment, appears in the background. These riflemen are flanked by a rifle
sergeant in a gray dress coatee with yellow
epaulets and red sash of his grade, and by a
company musician, identified by the black
collar and cuffs on his gray coatee, who has a
bugle instead of the rifle or drum carried by
the musicians of the rest of the foot troops.*
U. S. ARMY PHOTOGRAPH

The American soldier, 1827. PAINTING BY
H. CHARLES MC BARRON, FROM THE U. S. ARMY'S
"THE AMERICAN SOLDIER" SERIES

*The need for continued development and
research in the military arts in time of peace
was well recognized by the U. S. Army in the
period following the War of 1812. Partially to
meet this need, Secretary of War John C.
Calhoun proposed a "School of Practice."
Then, in 1824, the Artillery School of Practice
was established at Fort Monroe, Virginia.
Unlike modern service schools, which first
instruct individuals, the Artillery School
began by instructing an entire unit at one time.*

*In the center foreground of the above scene
is a captain of artillery, his branch designated
by the gold trimmings on his coat and by the
yellow pompom on his bell-crowned shako.
His rank is indicated by the gold chevrons on
each upper arm. Designation of rank by*
*chevrons for company-grade officers became
necessary when "wings" were added to the
uniform in 1821, making the previous
designation of rank by epaulets impossible.*

*To the right stands an infantry grenadier
company sergeant, in a blue coat with white-
laced collar, white "wings," and buttons
introduced in 1821. His grade is shown by a
white chevron on each lower arm. The red
pompom on his shako identifies him as a
grenadier. Beginning in 1825, each infantry
regiment included a grenadier and a light
infantry or rifle company, on the basis of new
tactics issued to the U. S. Army that year.
They were retained in the regimental
organization until the 1830's.*

*In the background a detachment of Artillery
School troops is drilling, headed by company
musicians in red coats with yellow "wings"
and with the national coat of arms on their
drums.* U. S. ARMY PHOTOGRAPH

The American soldier, 1836. PAINTING BY
H. CHARLES MCBARRON, FROM THE U. S. ARMY'S
"THE AMERICAN SOLDIER" SERIES

As the Western frontier moved across the
Mississippi River in the 1820's, it became
apparent that cavalry would be needed to
control the mounted Indians of the plains. To
meet this need, a battalion of mounted rangers
was organized in 1832 for one year's service.
This experiment was followed in 1833 by the
formation of the United States Regiment of
Dragoons (later to become the famous 1st
Cavalry). A second dragoon regiment was
formed in 1836. This became the 2nd Cavalry.

In the right foreground stands a junior officer
of the First Regiment of Dragoons in a blue
coat with a yellow collar hidden by gold lace,
yellow cuffs and turnbacks, and light blue
trousers with yellow stripes. The drooping
white horsehair plume indicates that he is a
troop officer, and the two gold buttons on the
gold-lace slash flaps on the cuffs denote his
rank of second lieutenant.

In the background the dragoons going out
on patrol are dressed in their distinctive dark
blue jackets trimmed with yellow lace. They
wear collapsible leather forage caps. They are
headed by their red and white guidon, to
which the word "Dragoons" was added by the
order of the Secretary of War in 1833.

In the left foreground is an ordnance
sergeant (there was one on every Army post to
care for the arms, ammunition, and other
military stores) in his plain blue coat and light
blue trousers with a dark blue stripe down the
side. His grade is indicated by the four
buttons on the yellow slash flaps on the cuffs,
by the heavy yellow worsted braid on his
epaulets, and by his red sash. U. S. ARMY
PHOTOGRAPH

The American soldier, 1847. PAINTING BY
H. CHARLES MCBARRON, FROM THE U. S. ARMY'S
"THE AMERICAN SOLDIER" SERIES

*The war with Mexico saw the major part of
the small Regular Army making its way
through deserts and tropical forests far from
home. Well trained and well fed, this Regular
Army did more than its share of fighting from
Palo Alto to Mexico City.*

*The horseman in the foreground of this
painting of General Zachary Taylor's troops on
the march in northern Mexico is a dragoon. In
spite of regulations, many cavalrymen wore a
yellow band on the forage cap. The distinctive
dark blue fatigue jacket worn by this dragoon
is laced with yellow and is the same as that
adopted in 1833.*

*Beside the dragoon is a first lieutenant of
infantry in the dark blue frock coat worn by
most officers on this campaign. He is wearing
the regulation dark blue waterproof forage
cap. His rank is indicated by the single silver
bar on his shoulder strap to distinguish him
from second lieutenants, who had no insignia
on their shoulder straps at this time. The light
blue trousers with a white stripe down the
side and the silver buttons on his coat identify
him as an infantryman.*

*In the background is a column of infantry-
men in light blue fatigue jackets and trousers.
These, with the dark blue forage cap, made up
the uniform of the regular enlisted infantryman in this war.* U. S. ARMY PHOTOGRAPH

The American soldier, 1855. PAINTING BY
H. CHARLES MCBARRON, FROM THE U. S. ARMY'S
"THE AMERICAN SOLDIER" SERIES

*Experience in the Seminole and Mexican wars
had demonstrated that campaigns in swamps,
forests, highlands, and on prairies had to be
waged in undress, or fatigue, uniforms. After
the Mexican War, many officers felt that the
full dress uniform adopted in the early 1830's
and retained without modification was too
expensive, complicated, and old-fashioned.
Consequently, they requested a change. Their
requests were heeded. In 1851 radical changes
were made in the style of the dress uniform.
The uniform coat with sloping skirts and turnbacks, worn since 1810, was replaced by a
frock coat, and the tall, stiff dress cap was
replaced by a cloth "gig" cap. Some of the
branches also lost their distinguishing colors
at this time. The infantry now wore light blue
as a distinguishing color instead of the white
it had worn since the Revolutionary War.
Dragoons now wore orange instead of yellow.*

*The mounted rifle units, over their strong
protests, now wore green instead of black and
gold.*

*In the scene above showing a battery of
light artillery in 1855, a first sergeant of the
light artillery is shown in the left foreground
in the new jacket issued for mounted troops in
1854, with red piping denoting light artillery.
His grade is indicated by the three bars and
lozenge on his sleeve and by the red sergeant's
sash. The red pompom on his cap and the red
stripe at the base of the crown identify his
branch — artillery. The letter on his cap
indicates his battery.*

*In the right foreground is a quartermaster
officer in the blue frock coat prescribed in 1851
for all officers. The buff welting on his trousers
and the "U.S." ornament on the front of his
cap identify him as a general staff officer. His
pompom, the lower two-thirds buff and the
upper third light or Saxony blue, identifies him
as an officer of the Quartermaster Corps.*

*In the background is a battery of light
artillery.* U. S. ARMY PHOTOGRAPH

Union Army uniforms of 1863, midway in the Civil War. Simplicity of style and subdued color is evident. In the left foreground is a lieutenant of the Corps of Engineers. An infantry first sergeant is in the right foreground. U. S. ARMY PHOTOGRAPH

Shown here are uniforms of the Indian-fighting Army of the 1880's. In the left foreground is a Signal Corps sergeant. In the center foreground is a captain of the 9th Cavalry Regiment. In the background are mounted troops of the 9th Cavalry.

United States infantrymen supported by Gatling guns charge the Spanish positions on San Juan Hill, Cuba, during the Spanish-American War. This shows the typical combat uniform of felt field hat, blue flannel shirt, and khaki breeches and leggings, worn by the U.S. Army at that time.

The Spanish-American War saw the last wartime use of the Army blue field uniform. In this painting of a field hospital a major of the Medical Department appears in the center foreground. In the right foreground is a field artillery private. Company litter bearers are in the left background. U. S. ARMY PHOTOGRAPH

This Philippine island scene of 1903 shows the khaki service uniform. The first lieutenant of infantry in the right foreground and the infantry sergeant in the left foreground are wearing the uniform with a coat. In the background, infantry privates wear the blue flannel shirt without the coat. U. S. ARMY PHOTOGRAPH

These were the uniforms worn by the U. S. Army in France during World War I. The officer in the right foreground wears an olive drab serge uniform with boots and carries field equipment. The machine-gun company first sergeant in the left foreground wears a wool olive drab uniform with spiral wraparound puttees. A gun crew appears in the background. All men are wearing the shallow basinlike British-type steel trench helmet. U. S. ARMY PHOTOGRAPH

Combat uniforms, European theater, 1945.
Shown here are members of the 5th Infantry
and 4th Armored divisions. In the center and
right background are two infantrymen, a major
and his radioman. In the left background is a
Sherman medium tank with crew.

A modern military policeman equipped for duty as a traffic officer. All equipment is designed to make him readily visible and to insure that his instructions are easily understood. U. S. ARMY PHOTOGRAPH

Regiments and smaller-size special organizations are authorized to wear distinctive identifying insignia. These consist of designs enameled on metal. Officers wear these insignia on the shoulder straps of the service coat. Enlisted men wear them on the lapels of the service coat and on the garrison (overseas) cap. Shown here is the distinctive insignia of the U. S. Army Band, consisting of the crest of the unit's coat of arms. U. S. ARMY PHOTOGRAPH

Shoulder sleeve insignia (shoulder patches) were first authorized during the latter part of United States participation in World War I. These insignia are of brightly colored textiles. Originally many were cutout patches of felt appliquéd on a background. Later the details were embroidered. Shoulder patches are generally used to identify divisions, corps, armies, and certain special units or organizations.

Shown here is the shoulder patch of the 101st Airborne Division. The basic design was approved on May 23, 1923. "Airborne" was added on August 28, 1942. The black shield refers to the Wisconsin "Iron Brigade" of Civil War fame. The mascot of this organization was an eagle named "Old Abe," which accompanied the men of Company C, 8th Wisconsin Regiment, of the "Iron Brigade" into battle. As originally organized, the members of the 101st Division came from Wisconsin. U. S. ARMY PHOTOGRAPH

PERSHING'S OWN

Drum major belonging to U. S. Army Band. The baton, white gauntlets, red and gold baldric or shoulder belt, gold aiguillettes, and high busby are all symbolic of his position.

Arms of the U. S. Army Band. *The red and white bars (stripes) displayed on the shield, suggested by the American flag, are eight in number, in allusion to an octave in music. The blue border of the shield, suggested by the chief of the field of the arms of the United States, surrounding the bars is used to represent the U. S. Army as a whole and to denote that the U. S. Army Band is the chief musical organization of the entire Army. This is further implied by the sword (symbolic of the Army) and the baton (symbolic of the band) and indicates the military nature of the band. The small escutcheon depicts part of the arms of the Rhineland and refers to the band's Rhineland campaign during World War II.*

The laurel wreath of the crest suggests honor and is formed in the shape of a lyre, the symbol of music. The large white (silver) star is taken from the branch insignia of the general staff and alludes to the fact that the band was founded in 1922 at the personal instigation of General John J. Pershing while he was Chief of Staff. The bugle horn, one of the earliest adopted for martial music, refers to the military nature of the band. Inasmuch as it is also the ancient insignia of light infantry, it denotes that the U. S. Army Band is a marching band.

The ribbon under the shield bears the honorary title of the band, i.e., "Pershing's Own."

eled, gold-rimmed oval bearing a projectile superimposed on the center of the crossed cannon. From 1901 to 1907, field artillery (mobile guns which could be rapidly maneuvered in the field) was identified by crossed cannon with a red-enameled, gold-rimmed oval bearing a gold wheel superimposed where the cannon crossed.

In 1901, Congress established the Army Nurse Corps, thus giving official status to nurses for the first time. The nurses did not, however, have the rank, pay, or other benefits of officers. At first they were identified only by their civilian nurses' duty uniform. Not until World War I was a military uniform provided for them.

Insignia for aides-de-camp to general officers was first adopted in 1902. This consisted of a gold eagle perched atop a shield with a blue field and seven white and six red vertical stripes. The shield was edged in gold and the number of stars in the field indicated the rank of the general whom the aide-de-camp served.

In the same year the Medical Department adopted as its insignia the traditional sign of the medical profession, the caduceus, or staff of Mercury, with serpents intertwined about it. This particular device was first used in the United States Army in 1851 in order to identify enlisted hospital stewards. At that time commissioned officers of the Medical Department wore as a hat device the same insignia as other staff officers — the letters "U.S." in silver within a gold wreath. On their dress epaulets they wore the letters "M.S." in silver within a gold wreath. The caduceus insignia is worn today by medical officers and officers of the various corps within the Of-

fice of the Surgeon General. An identifying initial is superimposed upon it: "N" — Nurse Corps; "D" — Dental Corps; "V" — Veterinary Corps.

The insignia of the General Staff Corps, created in 1904, consists of a gold-edged, red, white, and blue U.S. coat of arms superimposed upon a silver star.

World War I marked the end of uniforms in the old tradition in all countries. After the first few months of that bloody conflict, the profession of arms no longer was romantic. In the first of the modern technical wars, uniforms which blended into the background became a necessity. The Germans adopted a gray-green uniform, the French a "horizon blue," the British and Americans an olive drab. Dress uniforms were laid away in mothballs.

Service dress with some modified details was now prescribed for all occasions. Enlisted men wore a dull bronze disk on each side of the standing collar. The disk on the right side bore the letters "U.S.," the disk on the left the branch insignia. Officers wore leather leggings, boots, or, on occasion, high laced boots or wrapped spiral puttees. Enlisted men for a time wore laced canvas leggings, but these were soon replaced by the wrapped spiral puttees. Soldiers detested the puttees, for it took long experience to wrap them properly and they were impossible to handle when wet.

The service cap and hat still were worn occasionally, but the enlisted man's cap now bore a dull bronze disk with the arms of the United States superimposed upon it. These headpieces were extremely impractical for combat duty, particularly in the trenches. For combat duty, Americans wore

Doctors and nurses with their patients, Brest, France, 1918, showing the uniforms of that period. U. S. ARMY PHOTOGRAPH

a shallow steel helmet copied from the British. It gave little protection to the sides and back of the head and was inferior to the German trench helmet. For duty other than combat, a soft felt visorless and brimless cap, commonly known as the overseas cap, was worn. Officers wore insignia of rank on the front left, and the cap was piped in the branch color or colors. Enlisted men wore a small, dull bronze disk bearing the letters "U.S." on the left front of the cap. The cap of enlisted men was not piped.

When World War I began, American officers were wearing a plain brown leather belt about the waist. Soon, however, they adopted the Sam Browne belt from the British. It consisted of a belt attaching to the front and rear of the waist belt and passing over the right shoulder. It had been devised in the late 1880's by General Sir Samuel Browne, who had lost an arm in combat and sought a convenient way to carry his sword and pistol. American officers, like the British, found it practical and wore it for a couple of decades after

66

World War I Army nurses in duty uniform. This photo was taken at Camp Hospital No. *45, Aix-les-Bains, Savoie, France.* U. S. ARMY PHOTOGRAPH

World War I. Eventually, changes in weapons and equipment made it less useful and it became simply an item of dress. Meanwhile, policemen, bus drivers and high school drum majors used this style of belt and stripped it of all military character.

Tanks, introduced as a weapon during World War I, at first were organized as a special branch of the infantry in the United States Army. The insignia consisted of the profile of a Mark VIII tank superimposed on crossed infantry rifles. About the same time, the lowly second lieutenant at last

was recognized: his insignia, a gold bar.

The World War I "street" uniform for Army nurses consisted of a white shirt-waist with high, rolling collar, a dark blue Norfolk jacket with waist belt buttoned at the front, and a long, full, dark blue skirt. The coat had long skirts and wide lapels. Both the coat and the skirt were patterned after women's civilian suits of the period. The coat was fitted with four large patch pockets closed by flaps and buttons. All buttons were blue-black horn or composition. A wide brimmed fur-felt dark blue or

World War I Army nurse dress uniform. These four women at Hospital No. 29, Camp Hunt, Le Courneau, Geronde, France, are wearing the blue uniform prescribed for wear at that *time. The small inverted chevron on the lower left sleeve denotes six months' service overseas.*
U. S. ARMY PHOTOGRAPH

black hat was provided. This was worn indented in the Montana peak style or in the porkpie fashion, according to the whim of the wearer. Black kid gloves, black hose and black high-top laced shoes with medium heels completed a nurse's dress. Blue was chosen for the color of her uniform because of difficulty in obtaining enough of the olive drab cloth which was being used for men's uniforms.

Army bands continued to grow in number and improve in quality. General John J. Pershing, convinced that bands helped the morale of his American Expeditionary Forces, encouraged their organization and use.

Shoulder sleeve insignia was introduced during World War I. They were colored cloth designs relating to the unit's history, place of origin, or assignment. Such insignia was first worn unofficially by members of the 81st Division, who adopted a wild-wildcat, in black silhouette, appeared on a white background enclosed within a black cat as their distinguishing device. The circle. General Headquarters of the American Expeditionary Forces immediately recognized the value of allowing men to identify themselves closely with their units. Other organizations were directed to adopt similar identifying shoulder insignia, and the practice has continued to the present.

With the introduction of gas warfare in World War I, the U.S. Army's Chemical Warfare Service was organized. The insignia is a benzene ring superimposed in the center of two crossed retorts. The Chemical Corps, successor to the old Chemical Warfare Service, still uses it.

In 1913, a few officers who qualified as aviation pilots were authorized to wear a distinguishing device on the left breast. It consisted of a flying eagle clutching the traditional Signal Corps flags in its talons while suspended from a bar pin bearing the inscription MILITARY AVIATOR. The signal flags were appropriate, since all flying then was directed by the Aviation Section of the Signal Corps.

With the rapidly growing importance of military aviation, new insignia appeared early in 1917. Officers designated as military aviators wore a shield with field, stars, and vertical stripes upon which the initials "U.S." were superimposed between outstretched wings. This was the first of the famous pilots' wings. The "U.S." was in gold embroidery, and the shield and wings were in silver embroidery on a dark blue felt background. For a short time during the early months of World War I, enlisted pilots were authorized. They wore a four-bladed propellor between wings embroidered in white silk upon a dark blue felt background.

As shown here, the enlisted men's cap of the uniform designed immediately after World War I was considerably less ornate than that worn by the officers. The visor, cloth-covered in the British Army fashion, and the cap band were the color of the wearer's branch of service. Under the small U. S. coat of arms appeared the number of the wearer's unit.

U. S. SIGNAL CORPS

Winter uniforms, 1918, issued to troops serving in the Siberian campaign. The enlisted man on the far left wears a mohair overcoat and fur-lined cap with ear flaps. The second figure is an enlisted man (mechanic) wearing a short overcoat with fur collar and fur-lined cap. The third figure wears a fur-lined parka-type coat.

The fourth figure from the left wears the conventional long officer's overcoat (the stripes on the lower sleeve indicate the rank of major) and fur cap. The figure at the far right wears a sheepskin-lined overcoat. U. S. ARMY PHOTOGRAPH

70

Several changes were made in the design of the wings between August and December of 1917. One provided insignia for balloon and airship pilots and was the silhouette of a free balloon between wings. At first, observers were given the U.S. shield with a wing on the left side only. Later it was replaced by one consisting of the letter "O" with a wing on the left side. The single wing indicated that the wearer, although part of an airplane crew, was not a qualified pilot.

In August 1918, when the air arm became a separate organization under the command of the Office of the Chief of Air Service, its insignia became a vertical airplane propellor between wings. With slight modification, this was continued until a separate United States Air Force was established following World War II.

During December 1918 many of the ratings and specializations in the air arm were combined and new insignia authorized. These were of oxidized silver instead of embroidery. Then, early in 1919, the wings and shield were redesigned and all flying insignia since that time have been based on the 1919 design.

During the latter part of 1918, as a gesture toward saving material, it was ordered that chevrons were to be worn on the right arm only. Officers and enlisted men also were ordered to wear a small "V" of gold braid on the lower right sleeve for each wound. For every six months spent overseas, officers and enlisted men wore a similar "V" on the left sleeve. For every six months of service in this country, officers and enlisted men could wear a similar device in silver braid on the lower left sleeve.

This uniform was never adopted! Immediately following World War I a new uniform was designed and a few samples tailored. The design shows several markedly foreign influences, a result of our close association with European armies. The high-collared officer's blouse is decorated with colored tabs bearing the insignia of the wearer's branch of service. These tabs are edged with gold braid and are the color of the branch of service. The pointed cuffs are trimmed in the same color and are patterned after those of the U. S. Marine uniform. Insignia and buttons are brightly polished at a time when dull metal was still regulation. The cap is extremely ornate, the rank of the wearer determining the degree of ornateness. The cap worn by captains, lieutenants, and enlisted men also bears the identifying number of the wearer's unit on the front below the cap badge. U. S. SIGNAL CORPS

Winter service uniforms, circa 1926. U. S. ARMY
PHOTOGRAPH

5

From 1920 to 1940

Because vast stocks of uniform clothing were left over after World War I, no changes were made in the uniform until the 1920's Even then the changes were comparatively few. The issue of the blue dress uniform for enlisted men would not be revived for many years, except for a few specially assigned individuals. Officers would not be required to possess blue uniforms, except for a few serving in special assignments in Washington, D. C. Not until after World War II would the blue uniform again be required for all.

In 1920, when the Finance Department was established, the diamond insignia of the old Pay Corps was adopted. A year later the Militia Bureau (eventually to become the National Guard Bureau) was established. Its insignia is a gold eagle, representing the Federal Government, upon which crossed fasces, denoting the unity of the several states, are superimposed.

During this same period the so-called "Pershing style" cap was introduced. It had a wider flaring top and a more generous visor than those of previous caps. It served as a basic cap design until the green uniform cap was adopted following World War II. Bright brass buttons and insignia were adopted in the 1920's, replacing the dull bronze items then being worn.

Rank of noncommissioned officers was

Blue dress uniforms for officers, circa 1940.
U. S. ARMY PHOTOGRAPH

Uniforms for tank troops, 1941. The figure on the extreme right is wearing a padded helmet designed to protect tank crewmen. U. S. ARMY

PHOTOGRAPH

*Summer uniforms, 1942. The central figure
represents General George C. Marshall.* U. S.
ARMY PHOTOGRAPH

76

Typical uniforms worn by U. S. Army general officers in the field, European theater of operations, World War II. Shown here are generals George Patton, Omar Bradley, Mark Clark, and Dwight D. Eisenhower. U. S. ARMY PHOTOGRAPH

Officer's winter service uniforms, 1942. U. S.
ARMY PHOTOGRAPH

shown by medium-sized chevrons worn point-up between the elbow and shoulder. The shoulder patch continued to be worn.

The tailoring of the uniform, particularly for enlisted men, was greatly improved during the 1920's. During the winter of 1925–1926 the roll-collar coat was introduced. For enlisted men, olive drab serge replaced the coarse olive drab wool uniform of World War I days. Officers wore uniforms of olive drab serge or elastique.

On each coat collar, above the notch, officers wore a bright brass or gilt "U.S." with the branch insignia below. Enlisted men wore a "U.S." on a disk on the right collar and a disk bearing the branch insignia on the left, all above the lapel notch and all in bright brass. Colored felt disks in the color of the wearer's branch were introduced for wear under the enlisted men's lapel and cap insignia, in an attempt to brighten a rather drab uniform. Officers wore a colored felt disk under their rank insignia on the overseas cap, which would be known hereafter as a garrison cap.

The garrison cap for enlisted men was trimmed with piping the color of the wearer's branch. Warrant officers wore piping of intertwined silver and black. Commissioned officers wore gold and black piping. Generals wore all-gold piping.

The wide-brimmed campaign or field hat of olive drab felt was retained for wear in the field. As in the past, it had a cord and acorns.

During the 1920's distinguishing devices were authorized for regiments and similar organizations. These are in the form of colored enameled devices, usually a shield bearing a coat of arms. Officers wear them

Women's Army Auxiliary Corps uniforms, 1943. To the left is Colonel Oveta Culp Hobby, first director of the organization, wearing the two-tone uniform of the period. The next figure is wearing the officers' winter wool olive drab. The third from the left is wearing the wool crepe off-duty dress. The figure at the right wears the wool olive drab uniform of enlisted members of the WAAC. The cylindrical cap with flap visor was popularly known as a "Hobby Hat." The eagle cap plate was often referred to as a "buzzard."
U. S. ARMY PHOTOGRAPH

79

Uniforms, Women's Army Corps, circa 1943-1945. The uniforms, left to right, are: officers' tropical worsted; tropical worsted uniform with shirtwaist; exercise suit with sweater and fatigue hat; fatigue, or working, uniform for cooks, bakers and laundresses, and cook's uniform. U. S. ARMY PHOTOGRAPH

on the shoulder straps and enlisted men on the lapel.

The use of distinguishing devices has now become so extensive and so complex that the Army has established a special heraldic organization to pass upon the design of all before they are authorized for use. The laws of heraldic design are strictly enforced.

The grade of warrant officer achieved a new importance in the 1920's. For a cap device, warrant officers wear an eagle standing on a bundle of arrows, all enclosed within a wreath. For a time this same insignia, in a much smaller size, was also worn on the lapels, while no rank insignia was worn on the shoulders. Later it was provided that junior grade warrant officers wear a brown bar, rounded at each end and broken by a narrow gilt band across the center from side to side. Chief warrant officers wore a similar bar with a narrow gilt band through the center from end to end.

On duty all ranks wore breeches. Officers wore boots and spurs or leather leggings. Dismounted men still wore the clumsy, wrapped spiral puttees. Mounted men wore neat, laced canvas leggings faced with leather on the side next to the horse. For dress and off-duty wear, slacks were provided for all ranks. These were not issued to enlisted men, who had to buy their own. Officers' slacks and breeches were of a light color elastique or serge popularly known as "pinks."

With the coat, officers wore a white shirt and black tie. Enlisted men wore a khaki shirt and black tie. For field duty, the coat was not ordinarily worn.

In the tropics and during warm weather at other stations, officers and enlisted men on field duty wore cotton khaki shirts and breeches. For dress and off-duty, officers could wear lightweight cotton khaki or lightweight khaki-colored gabardine uniforms. From 1926 to 1938, embroidered wings were authorized for optional wear by authorized personnel in place of the oxidized silver wings.

In the 1930's the officer's wardrobe was expanded to include such *optional* items as a dress uniform, a special full dress uniform, a blue and a white mess uniform, and a white dress uniform. But none was as elaborate as those worn in the past.

With the exception of a belt, the full dress and the dress uniform were the same. A fancy belt with a gilt-gold buckle bearing an eagle perched on a bundle of arrows transformed the dress uniform into full dress. The belt was made of alternating rows of gold embroidery and silk the color of the wearer's branch, except in the case of generals, who wore an all-gold embroidered belt.

The full dress and dress uniform coat was a four-button, dark blue garment with four pockets and a roll collar. Pockets were closed by flaps with small buttons. All buttons were gilt. "U.S." devices were worn on the collar, branch insignia on the lapels. Shoulder straps with raised gold-embroidered edges surrounding a cloth field the color of the wearer's branch bore rank devices, all in the manner of the Civil War shoulder straps. On the lower sleeves were two narrow stripes of gold bullion or gold thread enclosing a narrow silk stripe in the branch color. Generals wore a broad gold stripe without colored silk.

Officers other than generals wore light blue trousers with stripes the color of the branch. Generals wore dark blue trousers with double stripes of gold lace.

A white shirt with turn-down collar, black four-in-hand tie, black shoes and hose, were worn.

The dark blue bell-crowned cap, similar in pattern to the service cap, had gold braid about the top and bottom of the cap band with colored silk facing between. The cap device was the arms of the United States in gilt-gold. Captains and lieutenants had a plain black patent-leather visor. Colonels, lieutenant colonels, and majors had gold-embroidered oak leaves decorating the visor. General officers had gold-embroidered leaves also on the visor and a band of gold-embroidered leaves about the cap band instead of colored facing silk. The chin strap was gold for all officers.

The special evening dress uniform consisted of civilian "tails," or evening dress, modified by the addition of military trim, ornaments, and insignia, including buttons, sleeve braid and shoulder knots. The trousers had twin gold leg stripes with colored facing silk between, except that generals did not wear the facing silk between the stripes. The cap was the same as that for full dress and dress. A white waistcoat with gilt-gold buttons, white shirt with wing collar, white bow tie, black shoes and hose, were worn with this uniform. A very full dark blue cape lined with the color of the branch was prescribed for wear with the blue uniforms.

Army nurse and Women's Army Auxiliary Corps field uniforms, circa 1943. U. S. ARMY PHOTOGRAPH

The blue mess uniform consisted of a dark blue waist-length jacket with colored lapel facings and gilt-gold buttons, dark blue waistcoat, white shirt with wing collar, black bow tie, light blue trousers with stripes the color of the wearer's branch (except that generals wore a double gold stripe), black shoes and hose. The same dark blue cap worn with the other uniforms was used with this outfit. Gold shoulder knots bearing rank devices and gold-lace sleeve decorations added color to the uniform.

The white mess outfit included a white waist-length jacket with gilt-gold buttons and gold shoulder knots bearing rank devices; white waistcoat with gilt-gold buttons; lightweight black tuxedo trousers; white shirt with wing collar; black bow tie; black shoes and hose. A white cap, decorated in the same manner on the visor as the blue cap, was worn with this uniform. Branch insignia in gilt-gold and colored enamel appeared on each lower sleeve.

The white dress uniform consisted of a white roll-collar coat with four pockets and gilt-gold buttons, white shirt with turn-down collar, black four-in-hand tie, white shoes and hose, and white cap. Rank devices were worn on the shoulders in the same manner as with the olive drab service uniform. Lapel insignia was worn in the same manner.

By the late 1930's, flying officers finally had given up the custom of wearing breeches, boots, and the Sam Browne belt. Instead, they were wearing trousers and a service coat with cloth belt and flat, square brass buckle. This coat style would be adopted by all branches just before our entry into World War II.

At this time nurses had only their one-piece white ward uniform and cap. For bad weather and outdoor wear, an officer's-type olive drab overcoat with broad lapels and cloth belt and an olive drab garrison cap were authorized.

As World War II drew closer, a more practical field uniform was adopted. This, with slight modifications and additions, would be worn through all of that conflict. For the first time our fighting men were provided with a sensible combat outfit. It appeared in different versions, depending upon where the soldier was stationed or whether he was a paratrooper, tank crewman, or combat infantryman. Basically this uniform consisted of a lightweight, wind-resistant jacket, shirt, trousers, and laced canvas leggings. A practical helmet and liner affording maximum protection to the head was adopted. When not in combat, the soldier wore only the helmet liner or his garrison cap.

A variety of footgear was available including shoes, laced boots, and laced and buckled field boots. During World War II the old high shoes and canvas leggings finally were supplanted by rugged but comfortable shoes with a wide, buckled cuff into which the trouser legs were tucked.

The tank, used to a limited extent during World War I, had been developed into a fast, hard-hitting, effective weapon. For a time, the profile of the Mark VIII tank of World War I, in keeping with tradition, was used as the insignia of the Armored Center — tanks now being referred to as "armor."

Women's uniforms, U.S. Army, circa 1943. From left to right: nurses' beige tropical worsted service uniform; Women's Army Auxiliary Corps (WAAC) officers' white cotton mohair service uniform; WAAC officers' khaki tropical worsted; WAAC seersucker exercise suit; and nurses' beige one-piece summer dress.
U. S. ARMY PHOTOGRAPH

U. S. Army officers' uniforms, circa 1945. The officer second from the right is wearing the gray uniform of the leader of the U. S. Army Band. U. S. ARMY PHOTOGRAPH

As army aviation became increasingly specialized, a number of new ratings were authorized. Each aviation specialty had its own wings in combination with an identifying device. In addition to wings for pilots, there were wings for senior pilots, combat pilots, command pilots, service pilots, glider pilots, liaison pilots, bombardiers, navigators, aerial gunners, flight surgeons, flight nurses, and air crew members.

Just before America entered World War II, nurses were provided with a two-tone blue uniform which included a dark blue coat with gilt-gold buttons and light blue skirt. This was changed later to a two-tone uniform similar in general design to that worn by male officers — olive drab garrison cap, olive drab coat, and light tan skirt.

Army nurse uniforms, circa 1945. U. S. ARMY PHOTOGRAPH

Uniforms of the 1941 era. In the center foreground appear a brigadier general, his aide, a captain of field artillery, and a bugler of the 10th Cavalry Regiment. In the left background are two Army nurses. In the right background are cadets of the U. S. Military Academy.

6

From 1940 to the Present

The rapid expansion of the United States Army during 1940 and 1941 pointed up the need for a unified and centrally controlled military police organization. On July 31, 1941, the Secretary of War directed the Judge Advocate General to establish the office of Provost Marshal General and to create a Corps of Military Police. The military police, as we know them today, date from this time.

But military policemen are not a recent innovation by any means. From the beginning of military history, armies have designated certain selected men to perform military police and military law-enforcement duties. Interestingly, the office of Provost Marshal itself dates back to the Norman Conquest of England during the eleventh century. In those days the provost was a high-ranking officer personally appointed by the king to maintain the peace, safeguard the royal interests, and oversee the administration of military discipline. Gradually he assumed greater disciplinary responsibilities. By the sixteenth century,

In 1947 the combat infantryman wore a long jacket, wool trousers, and high shoes with buckled cuffs. His haversack, canteen cover, and cartridge belt were of heavy webbing material. The helmet, developed early in World War II, with minor modifications is still worn. This well-designed helmet gives excellent protection on the top, sides, back, and front of the head. It rests upon a lightweight liner which can be worn without the helmet as a field hat. U. S. ARMY PHOTOGRAPH

the Provost Marshal had become a permanent part of the military establishment, heading up a corps of his own. As early as 1611, a provost marshal was serving in the colony of Virginia.

At the beginning of the Revolutionary War, the Continental Army adopted, with little modification, the organization and titles of the Provost Marshal Corps of the British Army. Then, on May 27, 1778, Congress authorized a "Provost." This was an organization to consist of a captain, 4 lieutenants, 2 sergeants, 43 "provosts" or privates, and 4 "ex-carabiniers." The last-named 4 individuals were no doubt especially selected and trained marksmen who functioned as executioners.

This organization was raised to track down deserters and stragglers. In combat, the members of the Provost took up positions to insure that no soldier left the battle without proper authority. It was prescribed that members of this corps be mounted on horses and uniformed and armed as dragoons. It would therefore appear that the first military police uniform consisted of a blue coat with yellow facings, blue waistcoat, leather light brown or buff breeches, high leather boots, and a reinforced stiff leather "jockey" cap with flat visor.

Little is known about military law enforcement from the time of the Revolution to the Civil War. In 1862, however, a Provost Marshal General was appointed, and members of the Army were detailed to perform police duties under his direction. Following the war, the office of Provost Marshal was abolished, and any required military police work was performed by the various military units themselves.

During the early 1950's, Army enlisted men and women wore these uniforms. U. S. ARMY PHOTOGRAPH

With the advent of World War I, need again arose for a military police organization because of the large numbers of men mobilized and the complex nature of their deployment. For most of World War I, however, military police duties were performed by hastily organized units. No special uniform was provided. The only identification was an arm band bearing "M.P." in bold block letters.

Between World War I and World War II, military police duties were discharged by officers and enlisted men temporarily detached from their regular organizations for this special assignment.

Today, the present military police organization, formed in 1941, is a highly specialized and efficient corps. In the beginning it was manned insofar as possible by former police officers and security guards.

Uniforms of the 1951 era. A first lieutenant from the 25th Infantry Division is in the left foreground. A Medical Service private is in the right foreground. Signal Corps linesmen are at work in the background.

Training schools and high standards of proficiency were established. The organization has distinguished itself ever since.

The insignia of the Corps of Military Police consists of crossed pistols of the Harper's Ferry Arsenal Army Flintlock Model 1806 .54 caliber pattern. This was the officer's official side arm immediately following the Revolution, and it was the United States Army's first standardized pistol.

It was first proposed that the insignia be crossed police clubs — a part of the military policeman's equipment. At saluting distance, however, this insignia would have looked the same as the crossed cannon of the artillery branch. Next, the medieval mace or war club was suggested. But at a distance these looked like crossed potato mashers. Since military police were armed with the Colt .45 caliber automatic pistol, it was then suggested that it be used as the basis of the insignia. It turned out, however, that these looked like crossed carpenter's squares. Then the thought occurred that since the infantry branch used as the basis for its insignia the first standardized shoulder weapon — the Springfield Model 1795 flintlock musket — why not use the first standardized pistols for military police?

The distinctive device of the Transportation Corps was established in 1942. It consists of a ship's wheel (denoting sea transportation), surmounted by a standard U. S. highway sign (land transportation), upon which is a winged railroad car wheel (rail transportation).

The neat and popular Eisenhower jacket was introduced during World War II and was worn for a considerable period of

Enlisted men's olive drab winter service uniform, circa 1956. U. S. ARMY PHOTOGRAPH

Women's Army Corps uniforms, circa 1956. The enlisted woman at the left is wearing a taupe overcoat. The next figure is a second lieutenant in taupe service uniform. The third figure from the left is a first lieutenant wearing a taupe wool jacket and skirt. The enlisted woman at the right wears a taupe raincoat and hood. U. S. ARMY PHOTOGRAPH

time thereafter. Close-fitting yet comfortable, this waist-length jacket had two breast pockets and wide lapels. Officers and enlisted men wore lapel and rank insignia in the same manner as on the service coat.

Shortly before World War II, officers were allowed to wear a very dark green (olive green) coat, trousers, and shirt. This uniform continued through the war.

Three grades of technicians were created during this period. These were specialists who drew the pay of, but did not have the command authority of, noncommissioned officers. They wore a letter "T" under chevrons denoting their pay grade of staff sergeant, sergeant or corporal.

Every three years of service for enlisted men was indicated by an olive drab stripe on a dark blue background worn diagonally on the lower coat sleeve. For every six months of service overseas during the war, all personnel were authorized to wear a small gold-embroidered bar. These were first worn on the left sleeve, then were ordered to be worn on the right sleeve only.

A corps of women, the Women's Auxiliary Army Corps or the WAAC, was established in 1942. The members were uniformed in the same color as the men. The coat was of the same basic pattern as that worn by the men but was modified to fit the female form. Khaki was worn for summer and in warm climates, olive drab wool at other times. Women officers wore a tan skirt with the dark olive drab coat in the same color combination as that worn by male officers. A rather distinctive item of the WAAC uniform was the so-called "Hobby Hat," named for Oveta Culp Hobby, the first director of the organization. It was low, cylindrical, with a flat visor, and defied all attempts to make it look feminine. The distinguishing device of the WAAC and of Army women today is the head of Pallas Athene, Greek goddess of arts and crafts and known to the ancient Romans as Minerva, goddess of wisdom. As a cap device, the WAAC wore an awkwardly designed eagle known as the "buzzard."

In 1942, nurses wore a two-tone coat-and-skirt combination similar to that worn by WAAC officers. Nurses continued to wear the garrison cap and did not wear the Hobby hat.

In 1943, the WAAC was made an integral part of the United States Army as the Women's Army Corps or WAC. The Hobby hat was discarded and a feminine-style garrison cap was worn. Insignia of rank was the same as that of the rest of the Army and was shown in the same manner.

Among the new concepts developed during World War II was the use of paratroopers and rangers. Paratroopers, especially selected and highly trained, were equipped as heavily armed infantry. They were transported by air behind enemy lines and parachuted into position. The successful use of paratroopers by the German Army early in the conflict emphasized their value. Paratroopers wore a two-piece jump suit fitted with numerous large pockets in which to carry equipment and other gear. High laced boots, originally known as jump boots, were for a time characteristic of the paratrooper alone. They proved to be so practical, however, that soon they were being issued to other combat units.

Army green cord uniform: *This uniform was authorized in 1959 for wear by officers, warrant officers, and enlisted women of the Women's Army Corps as a summer service uniform. Made of polyester fiber and cotton cord, it has tiny green and white stripes. The skirt has six gores with a slide fastening opening at the left side. The coat is hip length, with open collar and lapels, sewn-down pointed shoulder loops, short sleeves, four-button front closure with antiqued bronze military buttons. A cord-edged braid trim of Army green is on the collar and cuffs.* U. S. ARMY PHOTOGRAPH

93

Army officer's summer uniform, shown here worn by an Army medical officer and an Army nurse. U. S. ARMY PHOTOGRAPH

Rangers, trained as commandos to strike hard and fast into the rear lines of the enemy, were generally uniformed as other infantry. They were the forerunners of the Special Force troops of today.

One of the most colorful of modern United States Army units was the short-lived United States Constabulary. This was an elite organization raised for the express purpose of restoring law, order, and internal security to a demoralized and defeated Germany.

Constabulary units were made up of seasoned veterans drawn from armored cavalry outfits then on occupation duty in Germany. Their distinctive uniform included a helmet liner decorated with a blue stripe enclosed within yellow stripes. On the front was a yellow disk bearing the letter "C" crossed by a red thunderbolt. This same insignia was also worn on the left shoulder. Yellow neck scarfs were another distinguishing feature of this uniform.

The olive drab Eisenhower jacket, olive drab trousers, and laced boots were worn for service duty. For dress, officers wore a full-skirted coat and light tan or buff trousers. All members of the constabulary were heavily armed and were organized as a crack police outfit. Weapons included pistols, carbines, submachine guns, armed jeeps, and tanks. In 1952, as it became evident the German nation was finding itself, the constabulary was disbanded and the members returned to their original units.

In 1947, the Army Nurse Corps was given permanent status, as was the WAC in 1948.

The service uniform changed but slightly after World War II and on through the war in Korea, except for the fact that enlisted men were provided with better tailored clothing.

For a time miniature chevrons were worn by noncommissioned officers and specialists. Distinction was made between combat and noncombat personnel. The former wore dark blue chevrons on a gold background. The latter wore the colors in reverse. These small-sized chevrons were never popular and soon were replaced by the larger version without distinction between combatants and noncombatants.

During 1950, a new branch, Armor, was created as a continuation of Cavalry, which passed out of existence. The insignia of the new branch consists of the traditional crossed cavalry sabers upon which is imposed a front view of an H-6 "Patton" tank. The Armor branch included an amalgamation of then existing tank battalions with cavalry units.

In 1951, a taupe-color uniform of considerably more feminine design and appeal was adopted for all Army women.

The following year, infantrymen began wearing light blue piping on their garrison caps and a light blue disk under the ornament on the service cap. In addition, combat-ready units were provided with a braided blue shoulder cord.

After World War II, it became increasingly evident that a new service uniform was desirable. Millions of olive drab uniforms had been manufactured during the war. In addition to being worn by United States troops, they had been worn with appropriate national insignia by a number of our allies. With demobilization, large surplus stocks were used to clothe displaced

Special cold-weather clothing for wear by members of the Women's Army Corps and Army nurses in Arctic climates. U. S. ARMY PHOTOGRAPH

*Artist's conception of modern soldiers in
combat, equipped with M-14 rifles. The soldier
in the foreground carries a hand-held radio.
CH-21 "Shawnee" helicopters transport the
troops to the assault area.*
U.S. ARMY PHOTOGRAPH

96

Side view of enlisted man wearing battle gear.
U. S. ARMY PHOTOGRAPH

Rear view of enlisted man wearing battle gear.
U. S. ARMY PHOTOGRAPH

Integrated Combat Clothing System developed by the U. S. Army is based on the layering system, whereby garments may be removed or added depending upon climatic conditions and type of activity. Insulating qualities provided by this technique keep the soldier comfortable in weather ranging from temperate to Arctic. The outer of the several layers are overwhites for operations in cold-dry environments, consisting of trousers and fur-trimmed parka. Worn with the complete system are cold-weather insulated boots designed to keep the feet warm at temperatures of −65° F.
U. S. ARMY PHOTOGRAPH

Enlisted man's work (fatigue) and summer field uniform. U.S. ARMY PHOTOGRAPH

persons and others in liberated and occupied countries. Surplus stocks were also released for sale to civilians in this country and often were used for work clothing. Consequently, several million olive drab uniforms passed from the control of the United States Army. No longer was the former time-honored "O.D." (olive drab) the trademark of the American soldier. One

Officer's khaki summer service uniform. U. S. ARMY PHOTOGRAPH

Officer's green uniform. U. S. ARMY PHOTOGRAPH

of the essential characteristics of a military uniform — that it be distinctive — was lost. Furthermore, the old olive drab uniform had been designed for both garrison and general duty wear. But the qualifications needed in a modern combat uniform often deny style to a garrison uniform. It was decided, therefore, to give the American soldier a smart new uniform which would enhance the prestige of the Army and inspire pride of service.

After much testing of various fabrics and colors, a gray-green uniform was selected. It was a return to the color worn by the elite rifle units of the Revolutionary War, the War of 1812, and the sharpshooters of the Civil War.

Issue of the new green uniform was be-

99

Enlisted man's green uniform. U. S. ARMY
PHOTOGRAPH

Taupe raincoat for officers. U. S. ARMY
PHOTOGRAPH

gun in July 1957. Basically, the design of
this uniform does not differ greatly from
that of the old olive drab uniform, except
that the coat has no belt. General officers
wear two one-half-inch-wide black mohair
trouser stripes one-half inch apart, and a
black mohair sleeve stripe one and one half
inches wide on each sleeve, three inches
from the bottom of the sleeve. Other officers wear a one-and-one-half-inch black
mohair trouser stripe, and a black mohair
sleeve stripe three-fourths of an inch wide
in the same manner as generals. Enlisted
men do not wear these stripes.

This uniform is smartly tailored and the
American soldier today is one of the neat-
est, best-uniformed fighting men in the
world.

100

Taupe wool overcoat for officers. U. S. ARMY
PHOTOGRAPH

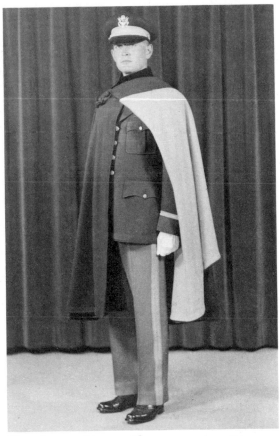

Blue dress uniform with cape. U. S. ARMY
PHOTOGRAPH

For dress, a blue uniform is now author-ized for individual wear by enlisted men and for government issue to men on special duty, including honor guards and bands-men. The coat is similar to that worn with the green uniform, except that it is dark blue and is worn with a white shirt and black tie (black bow tie for dress and four-in-hand tie for semidress). The shoulder straps are piped with gold-colored nylon or rayon. A one-eighth-inch stripe of the same material is worn about the lower sleeve, three inches from the bottom. The light blue trousers for all enlisted men have a gold-colored nylon or rayon stripe one and one-half inches wide. The dark blue cap and the green cap are alike in style, but the dark blue dress cap has a dark blue

Blue mess dress uniform. U. S. ARMY
PHOTOGRAPH

Army officer's white mess dress uniform. U. S.
ARMY PHOTOGRAPH

mohair band, with a gold nylon or rayon band one-half inch wide at the top.

Cap and lapel devices are the same for both blue and green uniforms. The arms of the United States on a disk, all in bright brass, is worn as a cap device. On the right collar, the letters "U.S." appear on a disk, and on the left collar, the branch insignia also appears on a disk in bright brass. Under each brass disk is a somewhat larger felt disk the color of the wearer's branch.

Gold chevrons and service stripes are worn on both the blue and green enlisted men's uniforms.

Blue, white, blue mess, white mess, and evening dress uniforms are authorized for wear by male officers. They are similar in many respects to those worn before World War II, except for a few details. Officers other than generals now wear a stripe of

Officers' blue dress uniform (in this case a major). Generally this uniform is worn when attending state functions at home or abroad when military personnel of other nations may be present in dress uniform, and on other occasions when common usage and good judgment dictate. It is worn at social functions of a general or official nature after retreat, for social use before retreat, for off-duty wear away from military installations, and when prescribed by commanding officers. U. S. ARMY PHOTOGRAPH

Enlisted man's blue uniform for dress and semi-dress. U. S. ARMY PHOTOGRAPH

Blue dress uniform for women. Enlisted woman on the left, officer on the right. U. S. ARMY PHOTOGRAPH

gold nylon or rayon on their light blue trousers instead of a trouser stripe in the branch color. A stripe of gold nylon or rayon is now worn about the lower coat sleeve, with no distinction as to branch. The sleeve ornamentation of the evening dress uniform has been changed to a single trefoil above a horizontal stripe extending around the outer half of the sleeve. This ornamentation is of gold lace, nylon, or rayon. Rank insignia is worn one-fourth of an inch above the horizontal stripe. General officers wear a blue-black velvet cuff four inches wide with a band of gold oak leaves about it. Above this band are the stars of rank. Brigadier generals wear 1 star; major generals 2; lieutenant generals 3; generals 4. The general of the army wears 5. These 5 stars are arranged in a circle with the inner points touching. Other general officers always wear the stars in a row. All sleeve ornamentation on white uniforms is of white braid.

For hot weather and tropical wear, a lightweight tan uniform is provided both officers and enlisted men. It is similar in design and tailoring to the green uniform, but it does not have a stripe, and the officer's sleeve braid is of khaki color. The green service cap or green garrison cap is worn with this uniform.

A uniform consisting of khaki shirt and trousers and the green service cap is prescribed for wear under certain conditions. An alternate uniform of short-sleeved shirt, shorts and green cap also may be worn as directed by commanding officers.

Black shoes and hose are worn with all but the white dress uniform, with which white shoes and socks are worn. A khaki

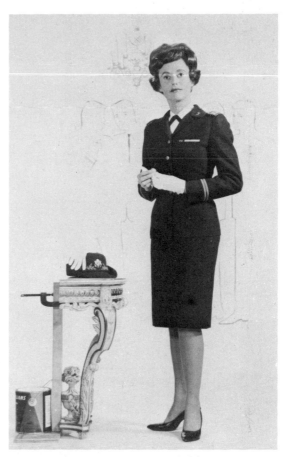

Women army officers wear this blue uniform for dress. The officer shown here has the rank of major. U. S. ARMY PHOTOGRAPH

Army enlisted woman's white hospital uniform.
U. S. ARMY PHOTOGRAPH

Army enlisted woman's green cord summer uniform. U. S. ARMY PHOTOGRAPH

shirt and black four-in-hand tie are used with the green and tan uniforms; a white shirt and black four-in-hand tie with the white and blue dress uniforms. A black bow tie and white shirt are worn with blue semidress; a black bow tie, wing collar and white shirt with the mess uniform. A white bow tie is worn with special evening dress.

Military police wear a blue brassard with the letters "M.P." in white on the upper left arm, laced boots, black pistol belt with black shoulder belt, black holster, policeman's club, white pistol lanyard, white gloves, and white cap cover.

Regulations now provide for insignia for aides to the President, the Secretary of De-

Army enlisted woman's beige summer uniform. U. S. ARMY PHOTOGRAPH

Army enlisted woman's green uniform. U. S. ARMY PHOTOGRAPH

fense, the Secretary and Undersecretary of the Army, and the Chief of Staff. The basic insignia is the shield and eagle worn by other aides, except that the field of the shield worn by the aide to the President is blue and has a circle of 13 stars upon it. The shield of the aide to the Secretary of Defense is blue and bears 3 crossed arrows between 4 white stars. The shield of the aide to the Secretary of the Army is red and bears the arms of the United States in gold between 4 white stars. That of the aide to the Undersecretary of the Army is white and bears the arms of the United States in gold between 4 red stars. Aides to the Chief of Staff have a shield divided

Army personnel qualified as parachutists wear an oxidized silver badge consisting of a parachute with a pair of wings attached at the base. This distinguished device was first authorized during World War II. Senior parachutists wear a star above the parachute and master parachutists wear a star within a wreath above the parachute. U. S. ARMY PHOTOGRAPH

diagonally from the lower left to the upper right. The upper part is red, the lower part white. This shield bears a silver star surmounted by the arms of the United States in color between 2 white stars at the top and 2 red stars at the bottom.

Warrant officers Grade 1 now wear a brown bar edged in gold broken by a gold stripe across the center from side to side. Warrant officers Grade 3 wear a similar bar, except that the stripe across the center is silver and the bar is edged in silver. Warrant officers Grade 2 wear a brown bar edged in gold with two gold stripes across the center from side to side. This divides the bar into three brown sections. Warrant officers Grade 4 wear the same bar except that the stripes and edging are silver.

Reflecting the changed character of its weapons, the artillery insignia of crossed cannon is now surmounted by a missile. During World War II the coast artillery was combined with field artillery to form a single branch.

The demands of modern warfare require troops especially trained in the skills of guerrilla warfare. This includes all military activities related to unconventional warfare, counterinsurgency, and psychological warfare. These rugged soldiers, known as the Special Service Forces, wear a dark green beret as a distinguishing item of uniform. On the beret is a special insignia of crossed arrows and a vertical knife within a ribbon scroll bearing the legend DE OPPRESSO LIBER, meaning, "freedom from oppression."

When General Pershing became Chief of Staff of the United States Army in 1922, one of his first actions was to order the

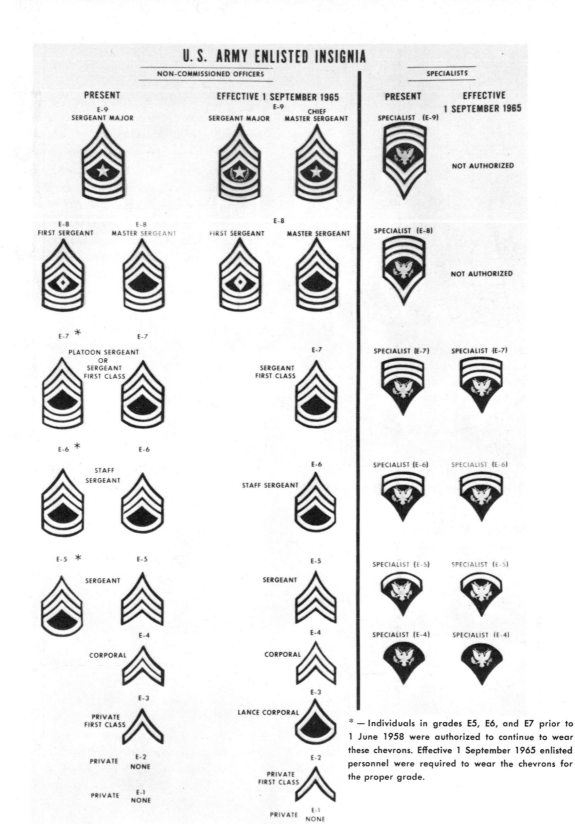

Present United States Army insignia for enlisted men. U. S. ARMY PHOTOGRAPH

The arms of the United States. This forms the basic design for the cap insignia for officers and enlisted personnel. U. S. ARMY PHOTOGRAPH

organization of *the* Army Band as distinguished from regimental and other unit bands. Especially selected musicians from the Army were ordered to Fort Hunt, Virginia, adjacent to Washington, D. C., where they were joined by outstanding civilian musicians enlisted for the new band. Soon the band was transferred to the old Army War College in Washington, D. C., now Fort Leslie J. McNair. The Army Band and the United States Military Academy Band represent the Army as a whole and wear special uniforms for dress. Organizational bands represent only their own units and wear the regular uniform with special trimming. The Army Band participates in ceremonies, state affairs, and special assignments, in addition to giving regular concerts in Washington.

Over the years the Army Band has worn a variety of special uniforms. For example, in the 1920's and the 1930's, it had a gray uniform. More recently, its dress uniform consisted of a yellow coat with blue cuffs, blue braid trim and blue shoulder knots. Blue trousers with yellow stripe down the outside seam and a blue cap with yellow band were worn with this coat. Though colorful, the uniform had little in keeping with tradition. So there was a return to traditional Army blue.

The present blue dress and full dress for the Army Band consists of a modified roll-collar coat with gold breast cord, shoulder boards and sleeve decorations, and blue trousers with double gold color stripes. Basically, the dark blue coat and cap and the light blue trousers are like those worn by other enlisted men for dress.

The drum major's dress coat, unlike that

of other bandsmen, has a stand-up collar. A metal lyre device in bright brass appears on each side of it. Instead of breast cords, he wears a gold-colored aiguillette on his right shoulder. About his waist is a gold belt with large bright buckle bearing the lyre device. White gauntlets and a high headdress with gold plume and cord decoration are colorful additions, as is a belt passing over the left shoulder. The shoulder belt, red with gold trim, bears miniature drumsticks and the arms of the Army Band.

The arms of the Army Band consists of a shield with horizontal stripes suggested by the stripes of the American flag. There are eight stripes, suggestive of an octave in music. Imposed upon the shield is a drum major's baton crossed with a sword, symbolic of the band and the Army respectively. A small shield, appearing in the upper angle formed by the crossed baton and sword, bears a portion of the arms of the Rhineland in commemoration of the band's World War II battle honor. Above the shield is a crest consisting of a lyre-shaped laurel wreath enclosing a star and bugle horn. The star alludes to the insignia of the General Staff Corps which General Pershing headed when he formed the Army Band. The bugle horn, the old light infantry insignia, suggests the military nature of the band. On a scroll under the shield appears the legend PERSHING'S OWN.

The elaborate dress of the drum major originated many years ago when, known as the "Whiffler," he marched ahead of the band to clear the way. In ancient times the drum major was a person of great authority. In addition to leading the band, he had the

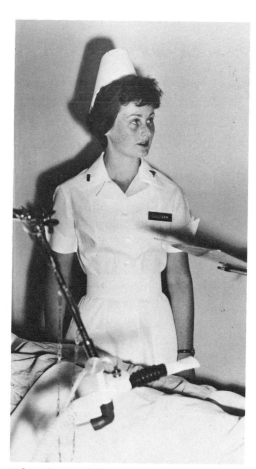

White hospital duty uniform of an Army nurse, 1965. SIGNAL CORPS

In 1950 a new branch called Armor was introduced into the U. S. Army. This branch was created as a continuation of the Cavalry, which has now passed out of existence. The insignia of the new branch consists of the traditional crossed cavalry sabers upon which is superimposed the front view of an M-6 "Patton" tank. U. S. ARMY PHOTOGRAPH

Master Army Aviator Badge awarded to personnel possessing certain prescribed qualifications as aviators. Senior army aviators wear this badge without the wreath. Army aviators wear neither the star nor the wreath. U. S. ARMY PHOTOGRAPH

responsibility of training the drummers, enforcing discipline, and acting as banker for the troops. As badges of his high office, he usually wore a high bearskin shako and a wide and colorful shoulder belt. His baton was his symbol of authority.

Today women members of the United States Army have a complete wardrobe of uniforms for any occasion, whether duty or social.

The green service uniform consists of a fitted single-breasted coat with easy-fitting hipline, a V-neck collar with rounded ends, notched lapels with square corners, and slanted side pockets with rounded flaps. There are four bright buttons down the front. Officers wear a band of one-half-inch black ribbed mohair braid three inches above the bottom of the sleeve. Officers' rank insignia are worn on the shoulder loops which extend from shoulder seam to collar. Noncommissioned rank is indicated by gold chevrons on the upper sleeves. The skirt is fitted at the hipline, so that no fullness shows below the coat. Besides an especially designed garrison cap, the women have a smart hat with brim turned down in front and up on the back and sides.

Officers' hats have a gold band about the crown and the arms of the United States on the front. Enlisted women wear the arms in smaller size on a brass disk. Commissioned rank devices are placed on the left front of the garrison cap. Lapel and collar devices are worn by the women in the same manner as by the men. Khaki shirt, black tab tie, black pumps or shoes, and appropriate hose complete the women's uniform.

Similar in design to the green uniform are white, blue, and beige uniforms. The officer's blue uniform is provided with raised, embroidered-edge shoulder straps in the same manner as male officers. A green cord uniform tailored as a short sleeved, two-piece suit is also provided for all women soldiers.

For optional wear, women officers have an evening uniform consisting of a midnight blue jacket, white silk blouse, black silk tab tie, blue cummerbund, blue headband, a straight skirt reaching to the floor, and black evening shoes. Sleeve ornamentation is similar to that worn by male officers. The headband is decorated with gold braid for captains and lieutenants, and with gold-embroidered laurel leaves for colonels, lieutenant colonels, and majors.

Combat and special skills badges are awarded to Army personnel. The Combat Infantryman Badge, awarded to soldiers for active ground combat, consists of a polished silver musket on a rectangular blue background in front of an oak wreath of oxidized silver. Subsequent awards are indicated by the addition of silver and gold stars at the top of the wreath. After the fourth award the musket is gold in color.

The Expert Infantryman Badge, awarded to soldiers who have passed proficiency tests, is a polished silver musket on a rectangular blue background.

The Army still operates its own aircraft on special missions and assignments. Men qualified as Army aviators wear oxidized wings, smaller in size and of slightly different design than those worn by Air Force pilots. A senior Army aviator has a star above the shield of his wings insignia, and a master Army aviator has a star within a wreath above the shield.

Parachutists wear an oxidized silver

Army regulations provide that "Identification badges are authorized to be worn as public evidence of deserved honor and distinction to denote service performed in specified assignments in the White House, in the Office of the Secretary of Defense at the seat of government, in the Organization of the Joint Chiefs of Staff, in the Office of the Secretary of the Army, as a member of the Army General Staff, or as a member of the Guard, Tomb of the Unknown Soldier, or a participant in the Army Student Nurse Program." Shown here is the Office of the Secretary of Defense identification badge. U. S. ARMY PHOTOGRAPH

Another of the identification badges is the Presidential Service Badge (formerly known as the White House Service Badge). This is worn by personnel assigned to certain duties at the White House. U. S. ARMY PHOTOGRAPH

Drawing of the identification badge worn by personnel in a position of responsibility under the direct cognizance of the Joint Chiefs of Staff. U. S. ARMY PHOTOGRAPH

badge consisting of a parachute with a pair of wings attached at the base. Senior parachutists have a star above the parachute, and master parachutists have a star and wreath above.

Qualified members of the Army Medical Service may be awarded the Medical Badge. This also is of oxidized silver and consists of a stretcher placed horizontally behind a caduceus and enclosed within a wreath. Second, third and fourth awards of the badge are indicated by one, two, or three stars.

Special identification badges are authorized as evidence of deserved honor and distinction and to denote service in special assignments such as the White House or Office of the Secretary of Defense.

Special uniforms are worn by the Honor Guard at the Tomb of the Unknown Soldier in Arlington Cemetery and by the Ceremonial Troops of the 1st Battalian (Reinforced) of the 3rd Infantry Regiment. This regiment, dating from 1784, is known as "The Old Guard."

The uniform basically is the blue dress uniform worn by all soldiers for dress. It is modified in several ways, however. The cap has a gold band just below the top and a smaller gold band below the cap band. A broad, thick strap of braided gold cord instead of the leather chin strap, is worn. The top of the cap has a trefoil design in gold braid. Gold shoulder knots replace the conventional cloth shoulder straps or loops. The cuffs of the coat are decorated with gold braid and buttons. A braided gold cord is worn about the right shoulder. The blue belt is edged with gold braid and has a gilt buckle. The trouser stripe on the

A distinguishing item of the uniform of the
U. S. Special Forces is this rifle green beret. It
is authorized for wear only by members of
Special Forces units and is worn with the field,
fatigue, and service uniforms. The Special
Forces insignia of crossed arrows with a
vertical knife superimposed and the motto
"De Oppresso Liber" (To liberate from
oppression) appears on the beret. U. S. ARMY
PHOTOGRAPH

The new "bush hat" now being worn by U. S.
troops in southeast Asia. U. S. ARMY
PHOTOGRAPH

Changing the Honor Guard at the Tomb of the Unknown Soldier in Arlington National Cemetery. The blue dress uniform has gold trim. U. S. ARMY PHOTOGRAPH

The Fife and Drum Corps of the 1st Battalion (Reinforced), 3rd Infantry Regiment (The Old Guard), wears uniforms and plays authentic tunes of the Revolutionary War period. Three members of the unit model the uniform, which consists of a black tri-cornered hat, black shoes with silver buckles, and white waistcoats, stockings, and wigs. The coats are red. The six-hole wooden fifes have no mechanical parts. The handmade drums have rope tension. The bugles are of a type used by the old light infantry. All of these instruments are patterned closely after those used in the 1700's. U. S. ARMY PHOTOGRAPH

Uniforms of the 1960's. In the left foreground is a master sergeant of the 1st Armored Division. In the right foreground is a major of the Transportation Corps. Enlisted men are in the background.

light blue trousers is dark blue edged with gold braid.

Members of the Honor Guard wear, on the left lower breast of the coat, a special badge consisting of an inverted open laurel wreath surrounded by a representation of the Tomb of the Unknown Soldier. The base bears the words HONOR GUARD in low relief. On the left shoulder of the coat, just below the seam, is a cloth arc also bearing the words HONOR GUARD.

The Fife and Drum Corps of the Old Guard wears uniforms and plays tunes authentic to the Revolutionary War period. The black three-corner hats, white wigs, white waistcoats and breeches, and red coats are similar to those worn by fifers and drummers in the Continental Army. The drum major wears a large leather helmetlike headpiece decorated with fur (similar to the old light infantry cap) as a badge of distinction. He is armed with a pike, which in the eighteenth century was used both as an infantry weapon and as a mark of rank.

These Old Guard musicians play wooden six-holed fifes and handmade rope-tensioned drums such as were used in the Army in the Revolution. The fifes are unique in lacking metal parts. The bugles are of the type used in the eighteenth century to summon men to battle. Although modern Army marching cadence is 120 steps a minute, the Fife and Drum Corps marches at the old pace of 90 steps a minute.

It is appropriate that the modern United States Army, versed in nuclear warfare, retains this symbolic tie with its origin in the Revolutionary War.

The soldier of the future: *An experimental combat uniform designed for nuclear ground-fighting. Over his camouflaged coveralls, which are protective against nuclear radiation, the soldier wears flexible body armor. Protective gloves are attached to the coveralls. Covering the face and the front of the head is a protective mask. Attached to the wearer's helmet are special glasses which permit vision through fog, haze and darkness.* U. S. ARMY PHOTOGRAPH

Sources

In preparing this work on uniforms, considerable use has been made of the notes which the author has collected during many years as a military historian.

Special mention must be made, however, of the materials made available by members of the Company of Military Historians. This erudite organization of scholars and artists has within the past decade and a half developed a wealth of detailed information on all aspects of American military history. It it virtually impossible to do any research in this field without consulting the detailed work done by these experts.

Listed below are the principal published works consulted in the preparation of this presentation. A brief description of each is given.

AMERICAN MILITARY INSIGNIA, 1800–1851, Duncan J. Campbell and Edgar M. Howell. Washington, D. C., Smithsonian Institution, 1963. *A well-illustrated study of the subject. Highly authoritative in every respect.*

ARMY AND NAVY UNIFORMS AND INSIGNIA, Colonel Dion Williams, USMC. New York, Frederick A. Stokes Company, 1918. *Interesting and informative account of uniforms worn just prior to and during World War I.*

ARMY INFORMATION DIGEST. Washington, D. C., Government Printing Office. *A monthly magazine of trends and developments in the U. S. Army. The issues of December 1963, June, September and December 1964; and September 1965, contain interesting and useful information on uniforms and insignia. Many color plates are included. Other issues of interest are those of September 1963 and June 1965.*

ARMY LIFE AND UNITED STATES ARMY RECRUITING NEWS. Recruiting Publicity Bureau, U. S. Army, Governors Island, N. Y., April 1946. *This issue of a since discontinued monthly publication contains photographs of West Point cadets, soldiers of World Wars I and II, and black and white reproductions of several Ogden prints.*

ARMY OF THE UNITED STATES, Quartermaster General, U. S. Army. New York, B. M. Whitlock, 1890. *A series of forty-four color plates of U. S. Army uniforms commissioned by the Quartermaster General and painted by the renowned military artist, H. A. Ogden, was published in 1890. The series appeared in several versions, including one with a descriptive text by Henry Loomis Nelson, in lieu of the uniform regulations. Three new plates were added to the series in 1901. Seven years later, twenty-three more plates were added by Ogden and were published without text. Some technical errors in some of the earlier plates have been disclosed by recent research, but those showing the uniforms after 1861 are without serious error. These plates were long out of print and became prized collector's items. The series was reprinted in recent years under the following two titles:*

UNIFORMS OF THE UNITED STATES ARMY (1st Series), text by Henry Loomis Nelson; paintings by H. A. Ogden. New York, Thomas Yoseloff, 1959. *A faithful reproduction of the Nelson text and the first forty-four plates by Ogden of the Quartermaster General's Army of the United States.*

UNIFORMS OF THE UNITED STATES ARMY (2nd Series), text by Marvin H. Pakula; paintings by H. A. Ogden. New York, Thomas Yoseloff, 1960. *A very good reproduction of the remaining prints of the Ogden series, together with some of Ogden's preliminary sketches, supplemented by an interesting descriptive text by Mr. Pakula.*

CADET GRAY, Colonel Frederick P. Todd, USAR. New York, Sterling Publishing Co., 1955. *An excellent picture history of the United States Military Academy at West Point as seen through its uniforms. Contains, in addition to many photos and drawings, many color plates by Frederick T. Chapman, an accomplished military artist.*

HISTORY OF THE UNITED STATES ARMY, Colonel Addleman Ganoe, U. S. Army. New York, D. Appleton-Century Company, 1942. *This authoritative work is the standard history of the Army from its birth to 1942. Far superior to other such histories it contains considerable detail. Out of print for many years, this history is being reprinted by popular demand of military historians.*

ILLUSTRATED CATALOGUE OF ARMS & MILITARY GOODS OF SCHUYLER, HARTLEY & GRAHAM, 1864. Reprinted, New Milford, Conn., N. Flayderman & Co., 1963. *Very few copies of the original catalog are now available and these command premium prices. This excellent reprint is a most valuable source for uniform details of the Civil War period. The regulations for the uniforms of the U. S. Army, Navy and Marine Corps are supplemented with many interesting illustrations.*

INSIGNIA AND DECORATIONS OF THE U. S. ARMED FORCES. Washington, D. C., National Geographic Society, Revised Edition, December 1, 1944. *Valuable reference on insignia and decorations. Contains over 2,000 color reproductions, in addition to hundreds of black and white illustrations. Now out of print.*

LOOK OF THE OLD WEST (THE), Foster–Harris. New York, Viking Press, 1955. *Much interesting material on the uniforms of the Civil War, the Indian wars, and the Spanish-American War.*

MILITARY COLLECTOR AND HISTORIAN, Washington, D. C., Company of Military Historians. (Issued quarterly to members only.) *Every issue of this journal is of great interest and value to any serious researcher. Contains a wealth of documented and well-illustrated information on all aspects of American military history.*

SOLDIERS OF THE AMERICAN ARMY, 1775–1954, Frederick P. Todd. Chicago, Henry Regnery Company, 1954. *Interesting and important pictorial history of Army uniforms. Thirty-two color plates by Fritz Kredel. Material is well documented.*

UNIFORMS OF THE ARMY OF THE UNITED STATES, 1861, Washington, D. C., Smithsonian Institution, 1961. *A facsimile of the 1861 uniform regulations illustrated with contemporary official War Department photographs. An excellent introduction to uniforms of the Civil War.*

UNIFORMS OF THE AMERICAN, BRITISH, FRENCH AND GERMAN ARMIES IN THE WAR OF THE AMERICAN REVOLUTION, Charles W. Lefferts. New York, New York Historical Society, 1926. *This long-out-of-print study, with its many detailed color plates, is the acknowledged classic work in its field.*

The Company of Military Historians, Washington, D. C., publishes sixteen color plates annually (four plates quarterly) in its *Military Uniforms in America* series. These are very well executed and are based on exhaustive research. Distribution is limited on a subscription basis to members only. Occasionally plates from this series are available from military book dealers.

Two series of color plates are available from the Government Printing Office, Washington, D. C. which provide an excellent insight into the history of American Army uniforms. The *History of the United States Army* is a series of fourteen color posters showing significant action scenes in the history of the Army. Uniform details are excellent. *The American Soldier* series consists of two sets of ten color plates each. All are by H. Charles McBarron, Jr., probably the outstanding military uniform artist of our time. This most important series shows all major changes in the uniform from 1775 to the present time. *Reproduction of many of these plates are used in this book.*

Valuable information is to be found in various U. S. Army regulations through the years. Until around 1814, uniform regulations appeared in manuscript form. For many years after that date they appeared as Army General Orders. Until 1881 they also appeared in Army Regulations. From 1881 to 1925 they appeared as special publications. Recently they have again been a part of the Army Regulations. These and other materials on the Army and its uniform may be found in The National Archives, Washington, D.C.

Excellent pictorial material is lodged in the Photographic Records Division, U.S. Army Photographic Agency, The Pentagon, Washington, D.C.

Reference materials, including pictures, are also available at the Library of Congress, Washington, D.C.

Specimens of uniforms of all periods are in the Smithsonian Institution, Washington, D. C., and in the West Point Museum, West Point, N.Y.

INDEX

The Author

It is not surprising that Robert H. Rankin has absorbed himself in a study of military uniforms for many years. Now a Colonel on active duty with the U. S. Marine Corps, he formerly was an enlisted man and officer in the U. S. Army. Since high school, when he sold his first magazine article, he has published many articles and books on aviation and military and naval history. Born in Martins Ferry, Ohio, he is a graduate of Eastern Kentucky State College. At his present home in Falls Church, Virginia, he has a large military reference library and an extensive collection of arms, including helmets, rifles, edged weapons, machine guns and three cannon.

Dragoon helmet plate of 1800. This is the first known distinctive branch insignia authorized for the Army. It shows a mounted dragoon in the act of charging. THE SMITHSONIAN INSTITUTION

A symbolic portrayal of the U.S. Army's long and distinguished history